Crafting a **Meaningful**,
Memorable, and
Affordable Celebration

SARA COTNER

Voyageur Press

First published in 2013 by Voyageur Press, an imprint of MBI Publishing Company, 400 First Avenue North, Suite 300, Minneapolis, MN 55401 USA

Voyageur Press titles are also available at discounts in bulk quantity for industrial or sales-promotional use. For details write to Special Sales Manager at MBI Publishing Company, 400 First Avenue North, Suite 300, Minneapolis, MN 55401 USA.

To find out more about our books, visit us online at www.voyageurpress.com.

ISBN-13: 978-0-7603-4142-1

Library of Congress Cataloging-in-Publication Data

Cotner, Sara.
A priceless wedding : crafting a meaningful, memorable, and affordable celebration / by Sara Cotner.
p. cm.
Includes index.
Summary: "Whether your budget is $2,000 or $20,000, *A Priceless Wedding* has tips to keep fun, family, and friends at the center of the celebration."—Provided by publisher.

ISBN 978-0-7603-4142-1
1. Weddings--Planning. I. Title.
HQ745.C673 2012
395.2'2--dc23

2012024891

Editors: Margret Aldrich, Melinda Keefe, and Grace Labatt
Photo Researcher: Bryan Stusse
Design Manager: Cindy Samargia Laun
Design: Sandra Salamony
Cover design: Ellen Huber

Photographs by Nell Aburto: pp. 19, 101, 102, 123, 124, 126, 129, 145, 146, 166, 198, 203, back cover

Photos courtesy of the author: pp. 5, 6, 7

Photos courtesy of JeffLoveJessica.com: pp. 50, 130, 182

iStockphoto.com / digitalskillet: p. 82

Photo courtesy of Jessica LoCicero Photography: p. 104

Photo courtesy of Kimi Weart: p. 141

Altrendo images / Getty images: p. 168

Photo courtesy of Ruth Harper: p. 190

Shutterstock.com: 2, 3, 6, 9, 11, 12, 13, 15, 17, 18, 21, 22, 24, 25, 26, 27, 28, 29, 31, 32, 35, 37, 38, 39, 41, 42,45,46, 49, 51, 52, 54, 55, 57, 59, 60, 63, 64, 67, 68, 69, 70, 72, 73, 74, 76, 79, 81 83, 85, 86, 89, 90, 92, 93, 95, 97, 98,100, 105, 107, 108, 111, 112, 115, 117, 119, 120, 122, 125, 128, 131, 133, 135, 136, 137, 138, 141, 142, 144, 147, 149, 150, 153, 154, 157, 158, 160, 163, 164, 167, 169, 170, 172, 175, 176, 181, 185, 187, 189, 191, 193, 194, 196, 199, 201, 205

Printed in China

10 9 8 7 6 5 4 3 2 1

Contents

Special Thanks

It took a lot of hands to transform sixty-four avocados into enough guacamole to feed eighty guests at our wedding reception, just like it took a lot of input and support to transform ideas about how to plan a meaningful and memorable wedding without losing your savings or sanity into an entire book.

The list of people who deserve acknowledgement and gratitude makes me joyful:

To Matt Bradford, my partner in adventure and awesomeness, you are my perfect match. Whether we are running through sprinklers at a local elementary school, dressing up in Halloween costumes and delivering brownies to friends and local businesses, or hatching plans to celebrate our wedding with our friends and family, you inspire me to be a better person. I adore you. You are the chlorophyll to my leaf, and you are the reason this book exists. I am honored to have the opportunity to share our story.

To Henry Cotner-Bradford, my new baby boy, I appreciate your desire to take a nap every one and a half hours so I can write. When you are awake and I set the computer down, I enjoy the break provided by your laughter and your newfound ability to blow raspberries.

To Andy Dehnart, my longest-standing best friend (and the most desirable gay bachelor in the contiguous United States), I owe you big. You put enormous amounts of time and energy into analyzing the nuisances of the wedding industrial complex with me, and you didn't get frustrated when I started talking even more about weddings when my own was over. You simply pointed it out in your dry, ironic sort of way.

To Lynn Cotner-Rauh, my mother, who did not morph into Momzilla. Thank you for letting me forge my own wedding path, just as you let me forge my own life path.

To Chandler Klang Smith, the fairy godmother in my personal tale about how to go from a big dream to a published book, thank you for dusting off my proposal and working your agent magic.

To Melissa J. Bodeau, my writing partner extraordinaire, thank you for wrangling my words into something more presentable. I am indebted to you for your creative nonfiction prowess, meticulousness, reliability, openness, and passion.

To Ariel Meadow Stallings, the honest and courageous author of the book and blog *Offbeat Bride*, I bow down to you for being the pioneer of the movement to create weddings that truly reflect who we are, regardless of what others think.

To the many other bloggers who share their lives and inspire me to be more environmentally friendly, crafty, budget-minded, and connected to my community, and who convince me that I can achieve anything I put my mind to (with a little confidence and a lot of Internet tutorials), I do a dainty curtsey and a little twirl in your honor:

Katie at inoakpark.wordpress.com and abackyardwedding.blogspot.com
Sherry and John at younghouselove.com
Jordan at ohhappyday.com
Kristina at lovelymorning.com
Rubyellen at mycakies.blogspot.com
Andrea at www.superherodesigns.com/journal
Amy at progressivepioneer.com
Kelly Rae at kellyraeroberts.com
Meg at sewliberated.typepad.com

And then there are the kindred spirit readers of the 2000dollarwedding.com blog, who spent hours upon hours reading and revising drafts of this book. You added, deleted, replaced, and rearranged all sorts of things. Many of you were in the process of planning your own weddings, so I am immensely thankful (and indebted to you) for your willingness to carve out time for this project. You filled out survey after survey to share your ideas and your stories. Thank you for grounding me in the idea that it takes a village—to raise children, to pull off meaningful and memorable weddings, to write books. I owe you big hugs, cheek kisses, and a home-cooked meal.

And to all of you kindred spirits who read this book and uncover bits of inspiration: take it, make it your own, and please share your ideas with the rest of us!

We made up our own ceremony tradition to reflect our love of nature. We planted a live oak from my parents' backyard while our officiant talked about what it takes to nurture and grow a marriage.

Introduction

Matt and I got engaged because *The Nutcracker* was rescheduled and the University of Denver ice-skating rink was closed. As an alternative, I suggested, "Why don't we go out for Mexican food and plan a wedding?"

That was it. That was the proposal. It wasn't creative or flashy or sentimental. It was just life.

Matt and I had met two years earlier, right after Hurricane Katrina had ransacked New Orleans and a flood of evacuees poured into Houston. For three weeks straight, a group of local educators trekked to the Astrodome and corralled kids together for tutoring. We didn't have official permission to be there; we did it because the kids needed it. The disorganization and general chaos of the relief effort allowed us to walk right through the so-called security with two huge Tupperware boxes full of educational materials. "We tutor kids here," we stated with professional certainty. It worked every time.

My crush on Matt took root because of our daily fights about who should carry the aforementioned Tupperware boxes. Each of us insisted on carrying the containers for the group. He inspired me to be the one to step forward and say, "I'll take care of it."

Matt was always the last tutor to leave. "Where's Matt?," someone would ask as we squirted sanitizer on our hands at the Astrodome exit. "Oh, he's giving his kids a homework assignment. He said he would catch up with us."

Matt was also the tutor who was still running five miles a day, even though he had to be at work at 6:30 a.m. and we didn't leave the Astrodome until 8:00 p.m.

Matt was the guy with the sense of humor. When I told him I had recently read about the five languages of love, he remarked, "Yeah, I'm fluent in all five of them."

Matt was the guy who met my romanticized ideal: rugged *and* poetic.

After a few of those arguments about the Tupperware containers, I called two of my friends and said, "I think I found the guy I'm going to marry."

Five months after that, we returned from some nondescript outing or errand, and he blurted out, "I think we should move in together." I balked at how quickly our relationship was moving. However, after I spent three weeks studying Spanish in Ecuador, I realized how much I wanted to be close to him. He moved into my apartment when I returned.

The following year, we packed up our Houston lives and moved to Denver. Both of us wanted to get our Montessori teacher certification and teach in public Montessori schools. By this time, I had started wondering what our life would be like together if we tied the knot. Because I'm infamously indecisive,

We seized the opportunity to write our own ceremony so that we could share ourselves—including our sense of humor—with our nearest and dearest.

I just wasn't sure. We talked about what our lives would be like in the married future, and our friends started getting engaged all around us. I still wasn't ready to jump off the high dive.

One random day in the middle of winter, Matt came home with presents to relieve me of my seasonal sadness: a Chia herb garden and slippers from Walgreens. His gesture reminded me that I had never met a more thoughtful and hilarious person—a person I would be fortunate to call my life partner and the father of my (future) child.

We talked about how we would get engaged—if we got engaged. We would each plan a creative proposal and surprise the other person. I started coming up with my idea. It involved a website, so I went ahead and purchased the domain name www.ofafeather.us. I later found out that Matt, too, was coming up with ideas. His involved police officers and potbellied pigs running through our house.

Before any of our proposal ideas came to fruition, we were looking for something to do on a Friday night. We decided on a nearby production of *The Nutcracker,* only to discover it had been cancelled. Our second idea—ice-skating—didn't pan out either. In that moment, it didn't seem to make much sense to spend any more time and energy thinking about the proposal. It seemed much more practical to skip directly to the wedding, which is why I nonchalantly suggested Mexican food and wedding planning.

I started blogging about our wedding planning process as a way to work through our ideas and to keep track of what we bought and how much we spent. Since I had so few readers at the beginning, it was more like a personal journal.

Slowly, the blog's readership grew. And so did my insecurity. I was spewing out ideas left and right about how to make weddings more meaningful and memorable, and easier on the wallet and the earth. But what did I know? I had never planned a wedding before. I had no way of predicting how ours was going to turn out. What if all our ideas flopped? What if people were disgusted by our "tacky" and "budget" wedding? What if they didn't feel sufficiently appreciated for making the trip across the country because we spent too little on catering and alcohol and didn't splurge for welcome bags? What if all the modifications we made to the "traditional wedding" made it feel more like a wedding imposter than the real thing? It was bad enough worrying that our own wedding planning could result in disaster, but it was even worse worrying that I could be leading other people astray with faulty advice.

Planning our wedding was no easy task. First there was the logistical difficulty of coordinating a three-day event for eighty people without going into debt. Sure, I had planned birthday parties and potluck picnics, but nothing on that scale. Then there was the emotional difficulty of trying to break free of the traditional wedding mold and carve out our own authentic path. It's so hard when your best friend says, "What? You want me to cook at your wedding?" and your grandfather declines the opportunity to speak as part of your nontraditional ceremony.

Then there's the pressure that comes from the fairytales, magazines, TV shows, books, blogs, and consumer culture. Apparently a wedding just isn't a wedding without color-coordinated chair covers. There's so much cultural baggage about what makes a wedding a *real wedding*.

I get restressed just thinking about all that stress.

But in the end, our wedding was even more than we could have hoped for. It was the most perfect wedding *for us*. All the things we did to build community—from doling out jobs to making name tags with personal information—worked. No one got food poisoning from the fajitas we grilled ourselves. People played the board games we set out, soaked in the hot tub, told stories and cooked s'mores around the campfire, cried during our ceremony, and had fun drinking out of a keg.

Our wedding extravaganza started on a Wednesday with a family picnic high in the mountains of Colorado. I was with my Floridian brother when he experienced snow for the first time.

The rest of the week and weekend followed the same pattern of quality time with friends and family in a relaxed, outdoor setting. Every morning, we ate a leisurely and delicious breakfast provided by the B&B on a flagstone patio with our closest friends. For two hours, we sat beneath dappled sunlight, munching on scones, fresh fruit, and frittatas. I went horseback riding with my family and hiking with my friends.

On Friday the majority of our guests arrived, and we hosted a welcome picnic. Everyone helped themselves to a make-your-own sandwich bar, chips, watermelon, and homemade chocolate and cherry dessert with vanilla ice cream. People congregated in different areas to talk and connect. We had one friend teach swing dancing on the back patio. To combat the small talk conundrum, we fashioned name tags for our guests. Instead of "Hello, my name is . . . ," the tags read, "Ask me about: . . . " We listed three or four quirky things on each friend's tag. On our friend Camella's name tag, for example, we wrote, "Ask me about: Ashtanga yoga, raising chickens, DJ-ing a radio show, and why you shouldn't buy corn."

On Saturday, the day of the wedding, we spent a couple hours preparing food for the reception. A bunch of us piled into the kitchen to chop cilantro, tomatoes, and onions to make homemade guacamole, salsa, bean and corn salad, and fajitas. Other friends helped set up tables and chairs.

When it was time to get ready for the ceremony, friends pitched in there too. Beth did my hair, Marsha documented the whole event with her camera, and Marie packed drinks into the cooler.

The ceremony took place by a lake. My best friend officiated, and five of our friends and family spoke on our behalf. Then we planted a tree to signify the effort it takes to grow love, and we wrapped ourselves in a quilt, made from the fabric of family and friends, to signify the nurturing and support of our inner circle. We said vows to each other and the world.

At the reception, we dined on Mexican food in a grove of trees. After dinner and cake, we called everyone to the flagstone patio for "our first dance." Our wedding party stood around us in a semicircle. A friend announced our first dance and started the song. Then the entire wedding party broke into a choreographed dance while the speakers pumped out "Kiss" by Prince.

Then the general dancing started, and several guests joined us on the makeshift dance floor. Some guests played word games in the living room, while others hung out around the campfire. Several headed for the hot tub. I danced a lot on the flagstone patio, played a game, stopped by the fire, got in the hot tub, and mainly just chatted with my friends and family.

The festivities continued through Monday, with more leisurely homemade breakfasts and more time outdoors with guests. We were able to fully immerse ourselves in our wedding, to linger and relax into the comfort provided by good friends and family, good conversation, and good food.

The stress I had felt during the planning process dried up completely. I was able to be present in the moment and soak up every last bit of joy. I didn't worry about the fact that I never got around to hemming the vintage sheets we used for tablecloths. I didn't wonder if the napkin washer had done his job. Instead, I decided to let go, have fun, and rest assured that we would be married in the end—regardless of what happened.

After it was all said and done, I decided to write a book about weddings to help you and your partner plan *your* very best wedding. In this part memoir, part how-to handbook, I share how we (and others) resisted the pressure to create the wedding of someone else's dreams and instead forged our own path in a budget-minded, eco-friendly, handcrafted way. The book covers the basics of planning a wedding, from the proposal to the reception, securing a location, selecting an outfit, deciding on flowers, planning the ceremony, and choosing rings, as well as everything in between. Unlike other planning guides, this book focuses on how to reclaim the real purpose of a wedding: community, connection, commitment, and fun.

My hope is that this book will empower you to plan a wedding that reflects your values, to resist the wedding industrial complex, to cope with family pressure, to undertake do-it-yourself projects, to incorporate more green elements into the celebration, and to make your wedding meaningful and memorable—without losing your life savings or sanity.

I've included our story with the hope that insight into our thinking, wondering, planning, and compromising will be helpful during your own process. Each chapter starts with our experience and then addresses bite-size aspects of wedding planning, including things to consider, ideas, and insights from others. You can read the whole thing from cover to cover for a complete start-to-finish understanding, or you can use the table of contents to skip straight to a particular aspect of wedding planning. You can read about many of the kindred spirits featured in this book in the appendix and find more detailed information and templates at 2000dollarwedding.com.

It's been years since Matt and I slipped those eco-friendly, budget-minded rings on each other's fingers, and I'm still thinking and writing about weddings. I've come to understand that how we plan and execute our weddings matters. How we plan our weddings sets precedents for what kind of families we will be. How do we work with our partners to merge two different sets of ideas into something bigger and better? How do we disagree in constructive rather than destructive ways? How do we honor the input and experience of extended family members while simultaneously maintaining ownership over our own lives and choices?

Everything in life gets played out on the stage of wedding planning: independence, courage, compromise, communication, integrity, relationship building, letting go. There are times when you have to muster up the courage to assert your independence and say, "I understand that you want [insert any number of things] for me, but that's not what I want for myself." There are times when you recognize that your wedding isn't just about you and your partner, and you decide that compromising actually does make you happy. Weddings are truly a rite of passage; they are a chance to clarify our values and to live those values out loud.

It's the start of your new family. Here's to making it a good one!

TELESCOPE VERSUS MICROSCOPE:

Focusing on the Big Picture

Hooray! You and your beloved have decided to formalize your lifetime commitment. This chapter is the place to start. We don't focus on your wedding colors or ideas for bridal bouquets. We start with your wedding vision; we start by focusing on the big picture of what you value and how you want to share your love and commitment with your nearest and dearest. We offer a "Vision Setting Work Sheet" to help you get some ideas on paper, as well as directions for making a vision collage.

Part of developing your own vision is realizing that *there are no rules.* You can take or leave any aspect of the "wedding formula." Despite pressure from the wedding industry, indie blogs, family, friends, childhood fantasies, or cultural expectations about what a wedding has to be, you and your partner can craft the wedding that is just right for you. To plan your very best wedding, we talk about how to stay grounded throughout your engagement, including by developing wedding mantras. We delve into the deep issues of how to deal with imbalance during the planning process, as well as how to make sure your partnership is as strong as possible as you head into marriage. (We include a "Partnership Assessment" to help you focus on your strengths and pinpoint your areas for growth.) To get from vision to reality, we discuss the logistics of the planning process, such as specific strategies for getting yourself organized, planning the calendar, and building your to-do list. Every section starts with Matt's and my story and ends with specific ideas for next steps. By the end of this chapter, you will hopefully feel inspired and optimistic about collaborating with your partner to create the wedding of *your* dreams and have a plan for organizing your process from start to finish.

OUR STORY

Close friends of ours got engaged a few months before we did. By the time we baked a celebratory engagement cake and showed up on their doorstep, the bride-to-be had already purchased several bridal magazines and started a file folder to capture all her wedding ideas and inspiration. (Talk about organized!)

Instead of starting with the details—dress, flowers, centerpieces, invitations—Matt and I decided to try something different.

As teachers, we learned to create lesson plans though a backward-design approach. The idea is to start with the end vision first. You ask yourself, "What do I want students to know and be able to do by the end of this lesson?" Once you've answered that question, you can plan the smaller activities that align with the end goal.

Once I internalized a backward-design approach in the classroom, I started applying it to everything in my life. When I was planning my twenty-fifth birthday party, for example, I decided that my end goal was to have a fun party that made the world better. With that big-picture vision guiding me, I pulled off a "random acts of kindness" scavenger hunt and dance party with three different live bands.

Matt and I applied the same approach to our wedding. We wanted to figure out the big picture before we let ourselves dwell in the details.

Over chips, salsa, and a blank notebook, we brainstormed our overarching goals for our wedding:

- To have quality time with guests. We didn't want to follow the traditional pattern of having a few wedding "events," where the bride and groom have time only for a "meet and greet." We wanted more of a family and friends reunion. We also wanted to build community among our guests, since many of them would be meeting for the first time.

- To ensure that the experience didn't feel overly orchestrated. We wanted a celebration of our love, not a show. We wanted our wedding to feel deeply authentic and real.
- To conserve money. We didn't want our wedding to grow bigger than our marriage. Although our wedding was important to us, we agreed that it was only a brief celebration and not worth going into debt for. We also figured we could make the event special with sincerity, not money.
- To treat the environment right and stay connected to nature.
- To ensure the wedding represented us and our values as a couple by making all the decisions ourselves.
- To be relaxed and fully present.

In short, we wanted a wedding focused on community, connection, commitment, and fun in an eco-friendly, handcrafted, budget-minded way.

Agreeing on the big picture helped us stay grounded throughout the wedding process. Whenever we had to make a decision, we went back to our vision to check for alignment between the smaller decision and the end goal. Focusing on the big picture helped us weather the choppy oceans (and occasional seasickness) of wedding planning. When I became irrationally insistent on personalized photo stamps for our invitations, for example, a quick review of our six big goals helped me realize that our wedding would not be utterly and completely ruined if we went with more budget-friendly stamps.

We also wanted to infuse fun into our wedding. Matt and I gave ourselves permission to break from the standard wedding formula. We put each element of a traditional wedding under the microscope and examined whether we wanted to keep it or not. Here's a list of examples:

- A rehearsal dinner? Yes, because we want to spend as much time with friends and family as possible. But everyone will be invited, and we'll call it a welcome picnic instead.
- A ceremony on Saturday afternoon and a reception that evening? Yep, that makes the most sense because our wedding will be dominated by out-of-town guests. Plus, we're getting married in the mountains of Colorado, so we want to give people time during the day on Saturday to get out and enjoy their vacations.
- An officiant to lead the ceremony? Yes, but we want ourselves and our friends and families to do most of the talking.
- A ring exchange? Yes, we like the symbolism of rings.

- A wedding party? It sounds good to have close friends up there with us.
- A single-sex wedding party on each side? Nope. Some of my closest friends are males, and vice versa for Matt.
- A matchy-matchy wedding party? No. Our closest friends are already spending a lot of money to fly out for the wedding. We don't want them to feel obligated to fork over more money for attire.
- Traditional wedding readings? Not for us. We want our ceremony to be as original and engaging as possible.
- A religious ceremony in a church? That's what our Presbyterian and Catholic families would prefer, but we prefer to get married outside.
- Dancing at the reception? Of course! We love to dance.
- A first dance? Yes, but it's going to be an entertaining choreographed dance with the entire wedding party.
- A wedding cake? Yes, but only because we love cake. If we liked pie more, we'd go with that. If we were just so-so about cake, we'd have a dessert bar instead. But it doesn't have to be a tall, smooth cake. We're okay with a regular cake.

We decided to retain some elements of tradition so we didn't weird everyone out. I definitely wanted a white dress so it would be very clear that I was the bride. In retrospect, I wish I had had the courage just to buy the coolest dress ever (and continue to wear it for other occasions). I also decided that I wanted to hold a bouquet—not because it's tradition but simply because I thought I would be less nervous if I could hold onto something.

For the most part, we wanted everything to be on our own terms and for our own purposes, not because we felt pressure from anyone else. We had watched our close friends fall prey to the wedding industrial complex and didn't want to get caught in the same trap. Their wedding grew so big and out of hand that a month before they found themselves saying, "We just want the wedding to be over so we can relax on our honeymoon."

We wanted to truly enjoy our wedding and our wedding planning process. We didn't want to be so nervous or stressed out that our wedding just flew by in an instant. We wanted to authentically have a great time at our wedding, not just relive it through professional photographs of the day.

Although it was neither completely stress-free nor easy, we did manage to pull it off. We achieved all the goals we had set forth in our "Mexican Food Manifesto," and we even came in $38 under budget. Having a vision from the get-go helped immensely. Every time we had to make any type of decision, we referred back to our big-picture goals and decided accordingly.

The other element that helped us pull off the perfect wedding was staying organized. If we were going to plan a major event that spanned several days without the help of a professional coordinator, we knew we had to take matters into our own hands. We used a binder with dividers and punched holes in envelopes to make inexpensive pouches. We put absolutely everything related to wedding planning in one centralized place. We saved every receipt, printed out e-mail agreements, taped business cards onto paper, and even saved the tags from embroidery thread from our DIY projects so that we could match the exact color if we needed to buy more. We also had an Excel document with separate tabs to keep track of: things to bring with us to the wedding, the guest list with addresses, our budget, job assignments, the list of photographs we wanted taken, and so on. Everything we needed for wedding planning was at our fingertips, which helped us pull off a three-day event for eighty people without a glitch.

When I started to feel overwhelmed by everything that had to get done (we kept a detailed to-do list), I decided to write down the major tasks and spread them out over our seven-month planning process. We would focus on one or two things a week, which helped us stay grounded. We wouldn't worry about things that were scheduled later on down the line.

An authentic vision, plus a solid organizational system, plus a step-by-step plan, plus weekly to-do lists equaled a meaningful, memorable wedding with a healthy wedding planning process.

START WITH THE BIG PICTURE

Starting with the big picture is certainly easier said than done. I think one reason wedding planning usually starts with the details is because they require less of an investment—the stakes just aren't as high. Thinking about colors or dress styles doesn't require too much thought; it can even be relaxing. Trying to figure out what a wedding means to you and your partner, however, is much harder.

Imagine that it's two days after your wedding. Perhaps you're hiking through the rainforest in Ecuador or sipping a frozen daiquiri while gazing out over the Caribbean. Or maybe you're sitting on the floor in the middle of your living room, sifting through piles of gifts. What is it that you want to be able to say about your wedding when it's all said and done?

This question—the answer to which is your end vision—is *the* place to start when planning your wedding. It's a way to "keep your eye on the prize." If you have a clear vision of where you're going, you can make more strategic, smarter choices about how to get there. It's so easy to get sidetracked by detours. Leigh,

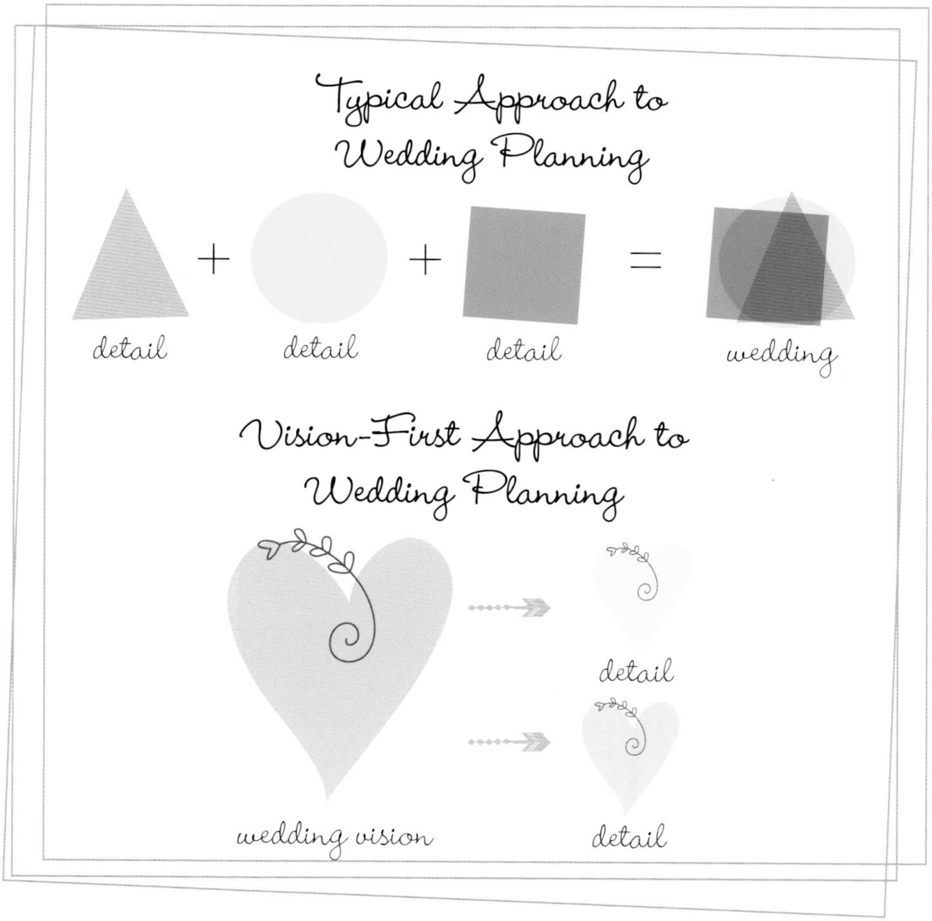

Typical Approach to Wedding Planning

detail + detail + detail = wedding

Vision-First Approach to Wedding Planning

wedding vision → detail

→ detail

a marketing specialist from Kentucky, has firsthand experience with this phenomenon. She explains, "Before we even got engaged, I was headlong into the fun house of wedding blogs. It took an afternoon of freaking out early into our engagement and making a list of precisely what we wanted our wedding to be for me to realize that the day is about us and our families and not pointless Internet validation. I'm still folding paper cranes and planning on a brooch bouquet, but I'm doing them for me, not to try and get a semblance of brief online wedding fame."

If you and your partner are able to define your vision upfront, you'll be less likely to get caught up in things that aren't connected to your end goal. Starting with the big picture, or the end vision, is a radically different approach. Instead

DIY Project 1:
VISION COLLAGE

It's easy to start with the details of wedding planning: centerpieces, music, flowers—oh my! But before you start focusing on the *what* of getting married, consider setting aside time to create a collage with your partner to represent who you are as a couple so you can stay focused on the *why*. A collage that encapsulates your relationship can serve as a strong visual anchor to help you weather the potential bumpiness of wedding planning (and can give you concrete ideas about how to share yourselves with your nearest and dearest during your wedding). You can pass by your collage every day and be reminded of your partnership and your upcoming commitment.

MATERIALS

Old magazines, newspapers, and catalogs
Sturdy paper with or without writing (pull something out of the recycling bin)
Scissors
Glue stick or rubber cement
Optional: picture frame

Tip: *When I make collages, I like to rip out interesting colors and patterns in large chunks. I glue those down as a background to cover up white space before I begin gluing on my selected words and images.*

DIRECTIONS

1. Start with your end vision by deciding how you want to display your collage. For example, if you want to store it in a frame, you can use the paper insert that comes with the frame as your backdrop. If you want to hang it on the refrigerator, you might want to use a sturdier background, such as card stock. Before you begin, decide what the ideal size is for your final collage and cut the paper accordingly.
2. This is the fun part! Flip through magazines, newspapers, and catalogs and rip out all the words and images that express who you are as a couple. What do you like to do for fun together? What words describe your relationship? If the process gets daunting, just start ripping out images you like. You certainly don't have to use every image you cut out. It's better to edit out images during the final stage instead of having to go back for additional images. Also, if you can't find the right words, consider piecing together letters to make words, ransom-note style. There's no right or wrong way to make a collage, so enjoy the process.
3. Once you feel like you have enough words and images (both to cover your paper and to encapsulate your relationship), neatly trim around the edges of each word and image and arrange everything on your paper.
4. Once you're happy with the arrangement, take off pieces one at a time and glue them down.

Display your vision collage in a place you will pass by frequently. It will help ground you throughout your wedding planning process and give you ideas about how to plan the best wedding for you.

Vision Setting Worksheet

This worksheet will help you and your partner create a vision for your wedding. You might also create a vision collage to represent who you are as a couple and to serve as a guidepost throughout your wedding planning journey. Setting aside time for big-picture planning upfront can save you a lot of time, money, energy, and grief later on.

What would you like to say about your wedding after it's over?

What would your partner like to say about your wedding after it's over?

What do you want guests to say about your wedding after it's over?

Which three words best describe you and your partner together?

Your List	Your Partner's List

What do you and your partner like to do together?

Where are your favorite places to go? Make this list exhaustive—it might help when you're deciding on a venue.

What do you like to do with friends? With family?

How do you want to spend your time in the days and hours leading up to your wedding, as well as in the hours and days following your wedding?

of letting all the little details add up to one big wedding, let your vision for the kind of wedding you want drive the decisions you make about the details. At various points throughout your planning, you'll come to intersections that offer up multiple ways to turn. If you have your destination in mind, you'll have a much easier time deciding which way to go.

THE WEDDING FORMULA

By the time you're ready to tie the knot, you've probably been to enough weddings to run through a detailed play-by-play in your mind. It might surprise you to know that many elements now considered "traditional" were manufactured relatively recently. So you aren't stepping on the toes of history if you want to change something. (If you want more in-depth information on this topic, I recommend the book *One Perfect Day: The Selling of the American Wedding* by Rebecca Mead.)

There's one concept that will help you through all the twists and turns of planning your wedding: There are no rules.

If you want your wedding to follow the standard elements of weddings in your culture, then by all means it should. But if you want to do things differently, that's okay too. It's a choice you and your partner get to make. Decide which

CROSS-CULTURAL WEDDING OPTIONS

If you and your partner come from different cultural backgrounds that celebrate weddings in unique ways, you'll have to decide which route makes the most sense for you. Options include:

- **Blend your two cultures into one wedding.** Incorporating aspects from both cultures can take different forms. You could bring elements of both cultures into every part of the wedding (the ceremony could have rituals from both cultures, the reception could have food from both cultures, and so on), or you could celebrate one set of cultural traditions during one part of the wedding (the ceremony) and the other set during a different part of the wedding (the reception).
- **Focus on just one set of cultural traditions.** If one partner is more attached to his or her cultural traditions than the other partner is, you might opt to celebrate just the one culture.
- **Plan two separate weddings to honor each culture in its entirety.** This option might especially make sense if you have family living in a different country.
- **Start from scratch.** Craft a wedding that is entirely separate from either of your cultural heritages.

elements of a traditional wedding you want to incorporate—because they represent what you like. Decide the elements you want to dump—because they represent others' expectations of what a wedding should be. As Victoria, an information professional from Vancouver, aptly put it, "Sometimes it's tough differentiating between 'what we really want' and 'what we think we want because everyone else is doing it.'"

It helps to remember that you have multiple options when it comes to any given element of a traditional wedding:

- Keep it (retain)
- Modify it (revise)
- Throw it out (reject)
- Make up a new one (reinvent)

Zinaida and her partner rejected all the "wedding clichés": groom's cake, bride's cake, mother-in-law cake, "millions of portraits and photo shoots." They opted for a wedding brunch, since brunch is their favorite meal. Right after their wedding, they took off their wedding clothes and went to the beach for swimming, kayaking, and paddle boarding with friends.

Abby and her partner are taking a different approach. She said, "Our wedding is turning out to be much more traditional than I'd initially imagined, but that isn't something I feel uncomfortable about—it's just surprising. I'm making deliberate choices and considering the input of both sets of parents, since this day is also very much about them."

When you internalize the idea that there is no right or wrong way to plan *your* wedding, you liberate yourself to find the path that makes the most sense to you and your partner—that is, your most authentic path.

THINKING THROUGH THE WEDDING FORMULA

The following worksheet will help you and your partner talk through some wedding formula elements that you might want to retain, revise, reject, or reinvent (bearing in mind that the "wedding formula" varies from culture to culture).

You don't have to complete this table in its entirety right now. The rest of the book will take you through many of these elements in detail; you can consider different options later. For now, just read through each element and see if you and your partner have any immediate thoughts about which ones to keep, modify, throw out, or make up from scratch.

One final thought: If you and your partner disagree about something, simply record both of your preferences. Now is not the time to engage in a wedding planning battle. We're just in the brainstorming stage.

Traditional Element	Retain	Revise	Reject	Reinvent
Formal white bridal dress	☐	☐	☐	☐
Bridal veil	☐	☐	☐	☐
"Something old, something new; something borrowed, something blue; and a silver sixpence in her shoe."	☐	☐	☐	☐
Garter	☐	☐	☐	☐
Bridal bouquet	☐	☐	☐	☐
Tuxedos for the groom and groomsmen	☐	☐	☐	☐
Same-sex bridesmaids and groomsmen	☐	☐	☐	☐
Matching dresses for the bridesmaids	☐	☐	☐	☐
Boutonnieres for the men	☐	☐	☐	☐
Mailed save-the-date cards	☐	☐	☐	☐
Invitation suite with an unsealed envelope inside the main envelope, invitation, reception card, RSVP card, and tissue paper	☐	☐	☐	☐
Wedding website	☐	☐	☐	☐

Traditional Element	Retain	Revise	Reject	Reinvent
Professional photography/videography	☐	☐	☐	☐
Rehearsal dinner	☐	☐	☐	☐
Religious officiant	☐	☐	☐	☐
Live instrumental music at the ceremony	☐	☐	☐	☐
Ceremony programs	☐	☐	☐	☐
Receiving line	☐	☐	☐	☐
Evening reception with a sit-down dinner	☐	☐	☐	☐
Assigned seating	☐	☐	☐	☐
Bouquet toss	☐	☐	☐	☐
Toasts	☐	☐	☐	☐
Dancing	☐	☐	☐	☐
Deejay	☐	☐	☐	☐
Official cake cutting	☐	☐	☐	☐
Guest book	☐	☐	☐	☐
Wedding favors	☐	☐	☐	☐
Formal exit	☐	☐	☐	☐

DISTURBING ADVICE FROM THE WEDDING INDUSTRIAL COMPLEX

"Your wedding is a show. Your obligation is to put on a show that impresses the women, period. Forget about the fathers, the brothers, the uncles, the male business associates invited—plan your wedding specifically for the women planned to be in attendance. Give the women a good show and your wedding will be a success, guaranteed."

—A news station in Oklahoma

THE WEDDING INDUSTRIAL COMPLEX

Weddings were once simple affairs that took place at home; expensive white wedding dresses were nowhere near the norm. Over time, the intimate, simple wedding sprouted and then grew (think kudzu) into a commercialized organism. When people realized there was money to be made off weddings, a whole industry emerged. Advertisers tried to convince everyone that they had to spend more and more money to buy more and more things to have a "once-in-a-lifetime wedding."

Enter the wedding industrial complex.

The wedding industrial complex (the WIC) is made up of all those businesses and vendors that make billions of dollars from manipulating excited (and then anxious) brides. The more the WIC can prey on couples' desires to make their weddings special and the more must-have items the WIC can turn into wedding traditions, the more money it can make.

Sadly, the WIC has shaped our cultural consciousness about what makes a wedding a wedding. According to the WIC, a *real* wedding includes an overwhelmingly long and expensive list of elements. There's nothing wrong with selecting items from the following list to craft a wedding that represents you. The specific items are not the issue. The issue is that the WIC tries to convince us that a "real wedding" must include all of the following:

Component	Requirements
 Big, white puffy dress	Must require more than one person to put on Must be difficult to move in Must pose a threat to your safety and well-being if you attempt to step backwards while wearing it Must require months of dieting and spandex undergarments to fit right Must require you to have another dress to change into for the exit Must require lots of money to be cleaned and preserved after the wedding
Flowers, flowers, flowers 	Must be held by the bride, the bridesmaids, and the flower girl Should also appear in corsages and boutonnieres Must be everywhere in the sanctuary: in big vases at the front, tied to every aisle, in baskets Must play a prominent role in the reception (centerpieces on every table)
 Big, tall cake	Must be very smooth and covered with fondant Must be cut during a ceremony in which the bride and groom stuff pieces in one another's mouth (in a clean or messy manner) Must have cute figurines that represent the bride and groom on top Must be cut with a cake cutter purchased specifically for the occasion

continued

Component	Requirements
Bridesmaids	Must wear expensive matching dresses that they will never wear again (except to parties that specifically require old bridesmaid dresses) Must wear matching jewelry Must wear up-dos (choose your bridesmaids carefully) Must all wear the same shoes
Invitations	Must be proceeded by engagement announcements and then save-the-date notices Must include many, many envelopes Must include a piece of vellum Must require more postage than an average letter
Rings	Must have a diamond engagement ring (a really big one) Must enjoy showing off and talking about your engagement ring at every opportunity throughout the wedding planning process

Component	Requirements
Reception	Must have a sit-down meal Must have cute table numbers and escort cards so guests can find their seats Must have an open bar Must have captivating centerpieces (don't worry if they prevent guests from talking to each other across the table; aesthetics are of the highest priority) Must have a live band or a deejay Must have dancing Must have a first dance Must have a bouquet and garter toss Must have a professional photographer and videographer capture the whole thing Must coordinate the exit, even if you're going to come back in and continue partying; it's important for the photographs

Miscellaneous

Must include other incidentals, such as:

Wedding favors

Gift bags for out-of-town guests

Facials for months leading up to the event

Tanning

Manicures and pedicures

Professional hair styling

Professional makeup

Teeth whitening

Guest book

Photo booth

Candy buffet bar

Aisle runners

Wedding garter

Veil

Unity candle

Dance lessons

Gifts for attendants

Gifts for parents

Menu cards

Bachelor and bachelorette parties

Rehearsal dinner

Postwedding brunch

Toasting flutes

Monogrammed napkins

Chair covers

The WIC makes billions of dollars by convincing couples that their weddings will not be "perfect" unless they put a checkmark next to every item on the list. Jocelyn, a full-time university student from New Brunswick, explains, "I felt a ton of pressure from the mainstream wedding industry (in the form of magazines, TV, online) to spend a certain amount on things, to include things that ultimately weren't important to us, and to basically follow a particular formula for our wedding. It took a while (and a lot of sane wedding blogs) to counteract those negative influences in our wedding planning process."

Leanore's wedding planning experience sheds light on the WIC. The woman she worked with at their venue was the president of a wedding vendor club "that schemed to raise the prices of sad, sorry services." The caterers she recommended were "way over budget ($40 a person for frozen lasagna on paper plates?)" and "TERRIBLE." Finally, Leanore's partner, Drew, sent out an e-mail to fifty caterers in the area stating what they wanted: $20 per person for everything, including food, setup, cleanup, and gratuity. A local restaurant responded, and Leanore and Drew realized that "staying off the beaten path rocked."

It's easier to deal with the WIC when its influence is overt. When a dozen flowers normally cost $10 at the grocery store, but it's going to cost more than $200 if very similar flowers are tied together for your wedding bouquet, you can see what's what and make decisions accordingly. However, the WIC is much more dangerous when it creeps into your psyche. Anne-Marie, a small business owner and educational therapist, describes it this way: "A part of me felt like I had to spend money for people to believe that I really loved my husband and am devoted to building a strong family with him." When she bought a $150 dress from Nordstrom to wear on her wedding day, she "felt apologetic" for not having a "fancier, more expensive gown." She and her partner decided to splurge on a $500 wedding cake because they were afraid they might regret it if they didn't. In the end, they realized they should have "bought a few pretty cakes" at the grocery store "and saved a few hundred dollars."

HETEROSEXISM AND THE WIC

"I'm one-half of a same-sex couple, so my entire wedding is basically a run-in with the WIC. In some ways, it's almost easier. I already don't fit the mold, so breaking it is already a given. In other ways, though, it's exhausting. For example, vendors are uncomfortable with us or don't know how to speak to us ("Will the groom also be joining you?")."

—Sarah W-W

Your best weapon against the WIC beast is simple awareness. Newly engaged Amelia put it best, "I am going in with my eyes wide open!" Once you're familiar with the characteristics of and tactics used by the WIC, you and your partner will be more prepared to step back and truly evaluate what makes sense for you.

"I picked up a few bridal magazines a couple weeks after getting engaged—as a joke, I thought. But, as I read them, this huge anxiety took root in my stomach. I knew, on an intellectual level, that I didn't want a wedding anything like what those magazines described. But I started thinking, Maybe everyone expects these things? Will my family be disappointed if there isn't a four-course catered dinner? Will my friends laugh at my homemade invitations? Thank God I had my future husband there to knock some sense into me."

—Tonya

BLOG-WORTHY WEDDINGS

In the second decade of the twenty-first century, a different kind of pressure is emerging: the pressure to plan the perfect "blog-worthy" do-it-yourself (DIY) wedding. That is, wedding blogs *might* cover someone's wedding, if it's "good" enough, whatever that means. (Blogging about your own wedding can be another stressor during planning.) Such weddings can be amazingly exquisite—awe-inspiring even! Everything is handmade, and the design and aesthetics are impeccable. Everything is coordinated, unique, interesting, and beautiful. Think picnic reception with individualized lunch boxes and cupcakes in Ball jars. Think rustic barnyard wedding with a live bluegrass band and glass decanters of homemade lemonade (with adorable labels, of course).

The problem with such blog-worthy weddings is that they set an impossibly high standard for the vast majority of us. They can pull our focus away from having a truly meaningful wedding. Instead, they make us preoccupied with how other people will perceive our wedding. We start to care more about how our wedding looks to outsiders than how it feels to those who are intimately involved with it.

Amanda, a Houston bride, knows this phenomenon all too well. She became obsessed with creating a blog-worthy wedding. She even had a specific wedding blog in mind. The process of trying to create a blog-worthy wedding became tiresome and stressful, however. At several moments throughout the process, she just "wanted the whole thing to be over." In the end, she was so fed up with her wedding that she didn't even submit it to the blog.

Weddings featured on blogs rarely reveal how much it costs to pull together such a detailed affair (both in terms of budget and stress levels). The expensive photographer and videographer narrowly portray the joy and aesthetically pleasing goodies.

Of course, there's nothing wrong with looking at these weddings for inspiration. The trick, however, is to remain self-aware about how they influence your own ideas about what's important. When necessary, close your computer and bring yourself back to the nonglossy real world.

THE ROLE OF DIY

I decided to make a tie for Matt to wear on our wedding day because I wanted it to match my dress (for symbolic reasons) and I wanted to save money (for practical reasons). However, when I actually got into the process of cutting, folding, and sewing, I realized that making that tie from scratch—with my very own hands—had more benefits than simply saving a few dollars. It helped me slow down and immerse myself in the moment, fully connect with what we were about to do and why, and feel an immense sense of accomplishment and pride. Handcrafting a wedding on a shoestring—despite the doubts of others—gave me a newfound confidence in my ability to dream big and make it happen.

As I see it, the benefits of doing it yourself are twofold. Of course, you can save money. Making your own bouquet from flowers that you buy at the farmers' market could save you hundreds. Deejaying your own reception with an iPod might save you thousands. But more importantly, a handmade wedding has the potential to be more meaningful and memorable. When you make something yourself, you feel more connected, proud, and fulfilled.

However, DIY can quickly become an obsession, a burden, a time and money sink, and a major stressor. When you factor in the money-saving potential of doing something yourself, you also have to factor in your time and your stress level, too. If doing it yourself is going to be incredibly time-consuming and stressful, perhaps it's not worth it.

Each time you and your partner are tempted to do something yourselves, consider the decision tree on the opposite page.

Some other questions to ask before you begin a DIY project:

- If you crossed this project off your list *entirely*, what would be the ramifications in ten minutes? Ten months? Ten years?
- How much will this project really cost (when you factor in the materials, time, and stress)?
- Is that cost worth it?

Only you know yourself well enough to know whether undertaking a project is going to bring you joy or unnecessary stress and anxiety. One reminder: Since there are no rules, there's nothing that says you have to have *any* DIY projects. If it's just going to be another "we should because someone else thinks it's important," revisit your vision and make a conscious choice that's right for you.

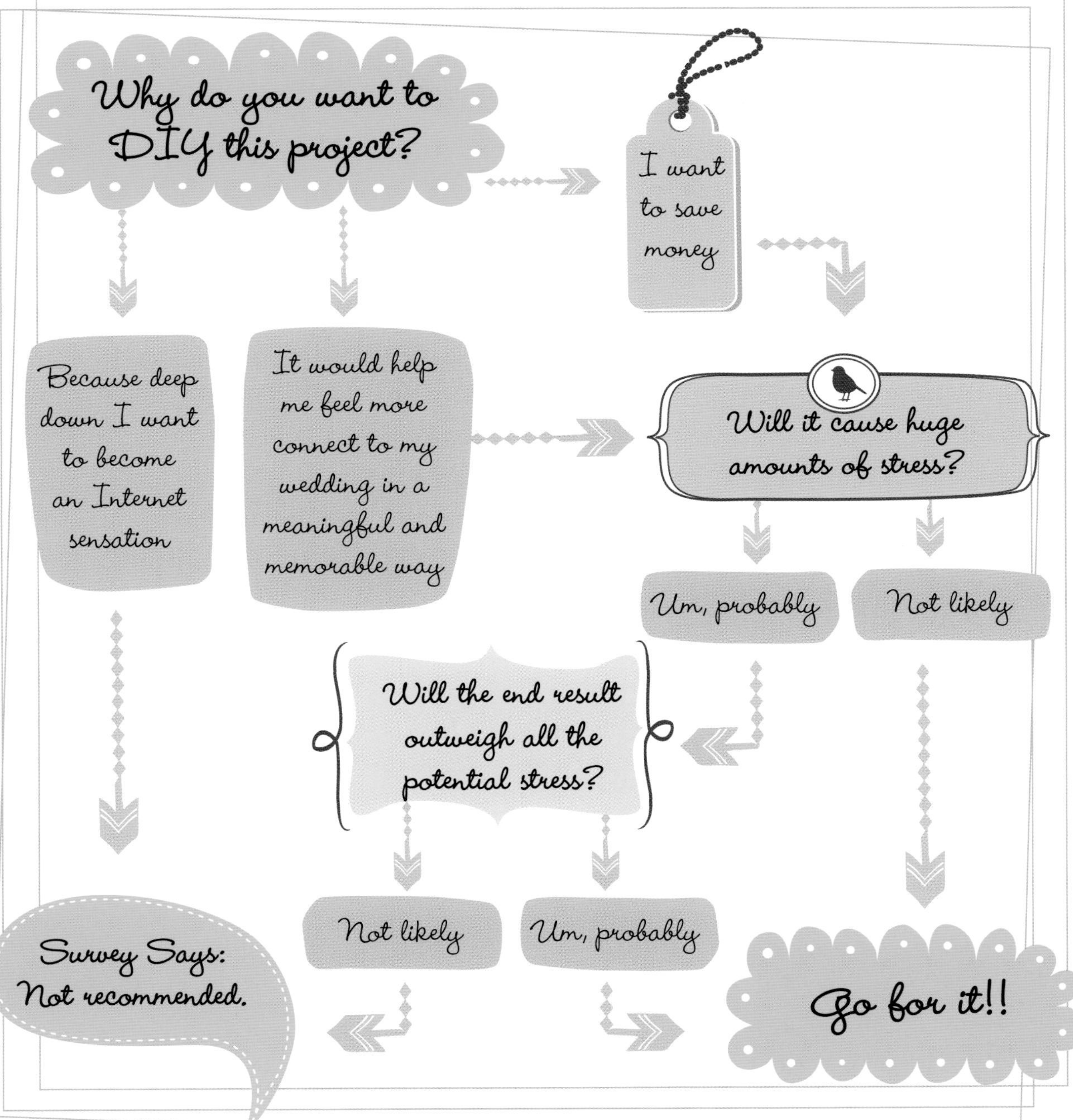
Why do you want to DIY this project?
I want to save money
Because deep down I want to become an Internet sensation
It would help me feel more connect to my wedding in a meaningful and memorable way
Will it cause huge amounts of stress?
Um, probably
Not likely
Will the end result outweigh all the potential stress?
Not likely
Um, probably
Survey Says: Not recommended.
Go for it!!

STAGES OF A DIY PROJECT

Sometimes DIY projects don't fall into easy, black-and-white categories. Throughout our DIY wedding, I found myself experiencing a range of emotions and reactions to specific projects.

STAGE ONE: PURE EXCITEMENT

The brainstorming, Google research phase is fun. So many ideas; so little time.

STAGE TWO: SELF-DOUBT

At times during the brainstorming stage, you might look at everyone else's stuff and wonder if you'll be able to make something half as good. If you have perfectionist tendencies, you might get mired in all the ideas and flounder a bit.

STAGE THREE: COMMITMENT

Your Jiminy Cricket voice reminds you that there's no such thing as "the one perfect thing" in arts and crafts. You decide on an idea and commit to it.

STAGE FOUR: PURE FUN

It can be relaxing and meditative to do crafts. You can reconnect with friends or family while you cut or sew or embroider. You can just think through your day or let your mind go blank and sing along to the stereo. You might think, "This is fun! I'm so glad I started doing this." In your highest moments, you start scheming ways to turn your craft into a business. You start thinking through the logistics of mass-manufacturing your creations.

STAGE FIVE: REGRET AND FRUSTRATION

Sometime in the middle of all the fun you're having, you start to realize that you have undertaken something that requires way more work than you realized. It's hard; it stops being fun; you're making mistakes. You might even ask yourself, "How much would someone have to pay me to make one of these for her?" Depending upon how deep into the stage of regret and frustration you are, your answer might be along the lines of a thousand or a million dollars.

STAGE SIX: SHEER PRIDE

And then the darn thing gets done. It's not perfect. It's crooked or smaller than you anticipated or not as comfortable as you thought it should be. But you are so proud of producing something useful with your own two hands. You might end up feeling more connected to yourself and the world around you. The best part is, you get to relive the sheer pride stage over and over again whenever you pass by the aforementioned craft.

Your DIY stages might look very similar or different. Just make sure that somewhere in the process, you experience a "fun" stage and a "pride" stage or a "seriously saving money" stage to make DIY worth it.

FOLLOWING YOUR OWN PATH

It's not just the wedding industrial complex and indie wedding blogs that will try to push you down a particular path. Nudges can come from family and friends, as well as from your own internal scripts about what a wedding should be. Whether you choose to go down one of these paths, tread on multiple paths, or forge your own, you should do so with intention and self-awareness. You don't want to get to the end of the process and think, "Where are we? How did we get here?"

"There were a few occasions now and then when family members would raise eyebrows when they would hear our plans—it just wasn't what they were used to. They had ideas in their heads of what a wedding was supposed to be (even my husband had some of these), but with a little talking, they began to realize that we didn't have to have a wedding 'by the book'—it could be whatever we wanted and reflect who we are."

—Heather Shoberg

It helps to wear shoes with good traction as you tread down the wedding planning path. You'll need to stay grounded. It also helps to think about your own personal process for being self-aware and for course correcting when you start to morph into someone you don't like or recognize. Do you journal? Think out loud while talking to your best friend on the phone? Work through things on long runs? Review your thoughts and actions as you lie in bed in the darkness right before falling asleep? Whatever your process is, you'll need to make time for it during this journey.

PREPARING FOR WEDDING PLANNING

I don't mean to be melodramatic and don't want to reinforce Bridezilla stereotypes, but wedding planning might make you feel a little crazy. Even the most rational, practical, level-headed people can lose it during the wedding planning process. You might find yourself bursting into tears because the save-the-date notices are slightly off-center (even if as a guest, you wouldn't notice).

There's something about the process that makes every little thing feel really, really big. Newlywed Diane explains, "Ironically, the wedding planning journey has been about the most UN-romantic period in our relationship. So much angst, so many unmet expectations. . . . It's all so, well, wrong!" She looks "forward to the aftermath, not obsessing over every little detail, and not turning every little unimportant thing into 'Oh no! This is all a terrible mistake!'"

Best-selling author Suzy Welch has a life strategy for staying grounded that can be applied to the potential craziness of wedding planning. She calls it the 10-10-10 Rule. When staring a difficult decision in the face, she asks herself what the consequences of a particular choice will be in ten minutes, ten months, and ten years. So if you think your wedding just won't be the same without, say, letterpressed invitations, a photo booth, or wedding favors, ask yourself how you'll feel with or without said item in ten minutes, ten months, and ten years.

I'm not saying that Wedding Planning Craziness (yes, it deserves to be capitalized like a syndrome) overtakes everyone. My hope is that you get through the process and think, "What the heck was she talking about?" But if you do find yourself in the middle of a wedding planning meltdown, rest assured that you are not alone. Hopefully, the ideas and perspective in this book will prevent some breakdowns. If you still find yourself in the middle of matrimonial meltdown, it helps to have as many tools as possible for dealing with it.

Enter the wedding mantras.

YOUR WEDDING MANTRAS

A wedding mantra is a short phrase that you can repeat over and over to help you keep your perspective and stay grounded. Here are a few of my favorite mantras:

- No matter what happens, we'll still be married in the end.
- Those who matter don't mind, and those who mind don't matter.
- A wedding is about community, connection, commitment, and fun—not about [list unimportant items that are causing you stress].
- Our marriage is more important than the wedding.

Take a few minutes to think about ideas and phrases that might help ground you during your wedding planning process. Feel free to fold down the corner of this page to reference this section, or write your mantas on sticky notes and post them on the fridge.

DEALING WITH IMBALANCE

Sometimes one partner is more gung ho about planning the wedding than the other one is. Maybe one of you wants to sit down and decide between "blush" and "bashful" for your wedding colors while the other just wants tasty food and good alcohol. Of course, those are stereotypes, but any kind of imbalance between you and your partner when it comes to interest in planning your wedding can lead to hurt feelings, conflict, and strife. Here are some ideas for dealing with imbalance:

FIGURE OUT WHAT'S CAUSING THE IMBALANCE

Is your partner less interested in planning a wedding because of underlying uncertainty about tying the knot? Does your partner seem uninterested in planning only when compared to your hyperinterest in planning? How you answer such questions as a couple will give you further insight into how to proceed.

ESTABLISH A WEEKLY MEETING TIME

If you think about the wedding all the time, but your partner isn't interested in taking up wedding planning as a hobby, then you have to figure out a way to get both your needs met. You need to get your partner's brainstorming and decision-making input; your partner needs to hear you talk about stuff other than wedding details every night. One solution is a weekly meeting to sit down and talk through wedding plans. You can collect your ideas and questions all week long and talk through them one by one during the meeting. Try to refrain from discussing wedding details too often (unless time-critical decisions have to be made) between meetings.

EQUALLY DISTRIBUTE RESPONSIBILITIES

Just because you might want to devote more time and energy to wedding planning than your partner does, doesn't mean you have to carry the load alone. You and your partner should agree on the responsibilities and divvy them up. Each of you should play an active role in helping your wedding come to fruition. Once you both agree on the assignment of tasks, record each task and its due date in a central location, such as on a document-sharing program or on the refrigerator. Posting the tasks and due dates can help you avoid reminding or nagging.

ENSURE THAT THE WEDDING REPRESENTS BOTH OF YOU

The best way to get your partner involved and invested in the planning process is to make sure that both of your tastes and preferences (especially when they're different) get represented in the wedding. Figure out what matters most to you and your partner and figure out how to reach a compromise that feels like a win for both of you.

APOLOGY OF A WEDDING-OBSESSED BRIDE

Dear Jo,

It's me. Your wife of three years, girlfriend of seven. And this is my long overdue apology for the wedding-obsessed creature I became in the couple of years before our wedding.

We barely knew each other when you proposed. I took it more as a romantic gesture than an intention; same-sex marriage was not legal, my family did not approve, and I hesitated before using such words as "lesbian" or "queer," like they were profanities.

Then you bought me a couple of wedding magazines. You probably thought they would make me laugh, or that I'd pin some of the pretty pictures on my wall. How could you have known what havoc a few glossy pages could have wrought?

From then on, instead of letting you bore me with current events or translations of Rilke, I now bored you with the finer distinctions between Alençon and Chantilly lace. I began using foreign words, like *chiavari* and *ruching*. I enlisted your help in weighing the merits of fuchsia versus berry, peacock versus turquoise. Because, dammit, we needed a color scheme. Don't you realize our color palette will inform every other aspect of our wedding? Stop smiling at me like that, Jo. Just because you live in jeans and plaid shirts and don't know lilac from lavender. Somebody around here has to care about the details.

On second thought, *obsessed* isn't a strong enough word. Make that *wedding-possessed*. Since we couldn't be legally married, everything, from peonies to place cards, had to be perfect. If we wouldn't have a valid marriage license, I'd be damned if the linens didn't match the altar candles.

We never set a date. My fault as much as yours. You wanted to wait until we lived somewhere with more than a month-to-month lease. And making a public declaration that I loved you scared the hell out of me.

Then same-sex marriage became legal in California, if only for a few months. You proposed, again. I didn't give you an answer. We bought a marriage license at the county courthouse, unsure if we would use it.

You found work as a field organizer with the No on Prop 8 campaign. The eighty-hour weeks meant we barely saw each other. You brought me home a campaign T-shirt, which I folded and put away without wearing; I had not worn crewneck T-shirts since I was eleven, when my mother cleared them from my drawers and made them into a quilt. I grew resentful of how little I saw you but was grateful for how easy it was to hold off answering your question; I realized I had spent months planning pew arrangements for an aisle I did not have the courage to walk.

One night that fall, I woke up to find you sleeping next to me, still in your jeans and "No on 8" shirt, your forearm thrown over your eyes. The light, faintly yellow as it often is when the moon is low in Los Angeles, fell in a bar over your back and showed me the violet-blue cast under your eyes.

I found the shirt you had brought me and threw it in the washer with every red sock I owned; it came out blush colored. I cut the collar off and cut the sleeves down to caps. I picked out a pair of earrings that matched the green on the emblem. I wasn't ready to say yes, but I was ready to let you talk me into it.

Our pastor married us on Election Day, the last day we could legally marry and the only day both you and he had fifteen spare minutes. The few witnesses from our church read from the Book of Ruth and played "Here Comes the Bride" on kazoos borrowed from the Sunday school. We both wore jeans and our "No on 8" shirts. My favorite lipstick was tucked into my coin pocket. And in that moment, with you holding my hands in that dim, undecorated sanctuary, I found that this love, stripped of all the lace and satin that had made it less raw and open and threatening to me, was what I wanted.

Forgive me for understanding the difference between cascade and pomander bouquets better than I understood why you were working sixteen-hour days. Forgive me for taking so long to realize that the shirt you brought me was more beautiful than the Ella Moss I would have chosen, because it means our wedding pictures will tell our children what we stood for. Forgive me for not understanding this sooner; I should have, because you are white and I am Latina, and less than fifty years ago, this would have been another reason we could not marry.

I'm not saying I don't still want a wedding someday. We both do. You want a wedding cake and to see me in a white dress. I want an excuse to carry around flowers all day and get you in a tux. We both want a big party with our family and friends. But I promise never to value mermaid gowns over marriage equality or aisle runners over equal rights. I promise not to give up. Our love may not be federally recognized within our lifetime, but I'm not going to bury that bitterness in letterpress and grosgrain ribbon.

I'm thankful you can't tell a French tulip from a calla lily. I'm thankful you can make electrical cable but don't give a damn about thermography. And whether or not we have a federal record to show for it, I'm thankful for you.

I'm thankful that we love.

Your wife,

Anna-Marie

KEEP THE LINES OF COMMUNICATION OPEN

If the imbalance in wedding planning starts to frustrate or sadden you, then by all means talk about it with your partner. In this way, wedding planning is good practice for handling the stress of marriage.

STAY SELF-AWARE AND GROUNDED

If your feelings start to get hurt because your partner doesn't spend enough time thinking about the wedding, ask yourself, "Am I spending *too much* time thinking about our wedding?"

My hope is that you get to the end of your wedding planning process and think, "Imbalance? What imbalance?" But if that's not you, then my hope is that you face the imbalance with grace, maturity, and proactivity (and assurance that you are not abnormal or alone). The conflicts we experience during the wedding planning process strengthen our relationships and better prepare us for marriage, which in the end is way more important than the wedding anyway.

PREPARING YOUR PARTNERSHIP

If you've been engaged for at least a week, you've probably already encountered "wedding checklists" that take you step by step through every detail that has to get done before "The Big Day." These lists rarely include the most important step: preparing your partnership for marriage. Our marriages are more important than our weddings. Our weddings are not just big parties with pretty decorations and expensive presents. Weddings formalize our lifelong commitment to another person. We can't lose sight of what they represent. We can't focus exclusively on the *what* at the expense of the *why*.

Alongside conversations about "What will our colors be?" we also need to talk to our life partners about things like:

- What kind of life do we want to create together?
- How will we go about creating that life?
- How do we nurture and maintain our individual identities while simultaneously building a life together?
- What interpersonal patterns have we learned from our families that will help or hinder our marriage?
- What things about our current relationship might change once we're married?
- How do we deal with stress and conflict in ways that will build rather than deconstruct our relationship?

THE BENEFITS OF COUPLES COUNSELING

I've always liked the idea of couples counseling . . . for other people.

When our relationship hit a rough patch, though, the first thought that went through my head was, "Oh God, don't only doomed couples go to counseling?"

Our rough patch took the form of me having a meltdown after not getting a surprise, fantasy marriage proposal after precisely three years of coupledom. For some reason, three years was my magic number, and when it didn't happen I went a little cuckoo (and mind you, I am not someone who thought I wanted to get married). Andy, my beloved partner, was on the five-year plan, not the three-year plan, so we decided to get some couples counseling to navigate this new landscape of thinking about marriage (and being on slightly different pages about it).

It took a few sessions, but slowly things started to get better. Our counselor helped us start airing our fears and grievances about marriage and started opening those oh-so-important lines of communication. One of the big points our counselor stressed was that our values are very similar and that with similar values you can work through a lot and stay happily together through the years.

The counseling went well—really well—and after four months, Andy asked me the big question (woo hoo!). That's when our counseling sessions officially turned into "premarital counseling" sessions. We made a list of topics we wanted to talk about, which included some of these fun favorites:

money
sex
religion
friendships
kids/parenting styles

We could have done this at home on our bed while eating Chinese takeout, saved some money, and not had to open ourselves up to a third party, but there are some really valuable aspects to going all out and seeing an experienced premarital counselor. Here are a few:

- You are committing to someone for life. Don't you want to know that he or she will show up to a counseling session during bumpy times?
- Counselors have seen around corners you haven't even thought of yet.
- Talking about important things can be easier when the discussion is guided.

I think the biggest reason I was reluctant to go through premarital counseling was that I was afraid we'd dig up some stuff that I'd rather leave hidden safely under the rug. Who wants to dig stuff up when you can throw yourself wholeheartedly into the high of being engaged and planning a wedding? But I chose to go through premarital counseling because marriage is about a lot more than a wedding day—it is about every day that follows the wedding day.

And, as we all know, the stuff hidden under the rug is going to come out eventually—and the longer it festers, the uglier it tends to be when it shows up.

Do you want to walk down the aisle knowing there are things you haven't really talked about? Or do you want to glow, from head to toe, as you walk toward your partner, knowing you are going to share your life with someone who will really show up for you—in a counselor's office, in a wedding ceremony, and in life?

—Kristen Walker

I recommend that every couple enroll in some sort of premarital counseling or class. Premarital classes help couples strengthen their communication, conflict resolution, and life alignment—all good things to have in place before saying "I do." Premarital counseling comes in all shapes and sizes, from religious-based classes to programs offered by the state. I recommend a class rather than self-study, because our best intentions can easily get lost in the shuffle of wedding planning. There's more accountability with a scheduled, consistent class.

If for some reason the premarital class route doesn't work out, there are good books that can guide you through the steps to strengthen your partnership, improve your communication and conflict resolution, and make sure you're on the same page about important topics.

I've also included a "Partnership Assessment" here, to help you jump-start the process. Set aside some time with your partner to individually complete the form. Then compare your answers as a catalyst for a conversation about the strengths of your partnership and areas for growth.

PARTNERSHIP ASSESSMENT

This activity is designed to help you and your partner assess some of the most important dimensions of your relationship. From the assessment, you will be able to determine your strengths, areas for growth, and next steps.

DIRECTIONS

1. Read each of the categories and think of specific examples from your life that help you evaluate the category. Use the category descriptions on page 44 to guide your thinking.
2. Rate each category on a scale from 0 to 10, with 0 representing an area for huge growth and 10 representing an area that is really strong and just needs to be maintained. Put a dot on the scale to indicate your evaluation.
3. Once you've marked a rating in each area, connect the dots.

SOME QUESTIONS TO CONSIDER

- What are your strongest areas?
- What are your most significant areas for growth?
- Have any ratings changed drastically in a relatively short amount of time?

- Did anything surprise you?
- Does anything worry you?
- Does anything inspire you to take action?
- What ideas do you have for strengthening your areas for growth?
- What are your specific next steps?
- Are there additional categories you would include?
- Are there categories you would delete?

Partnership Assessment

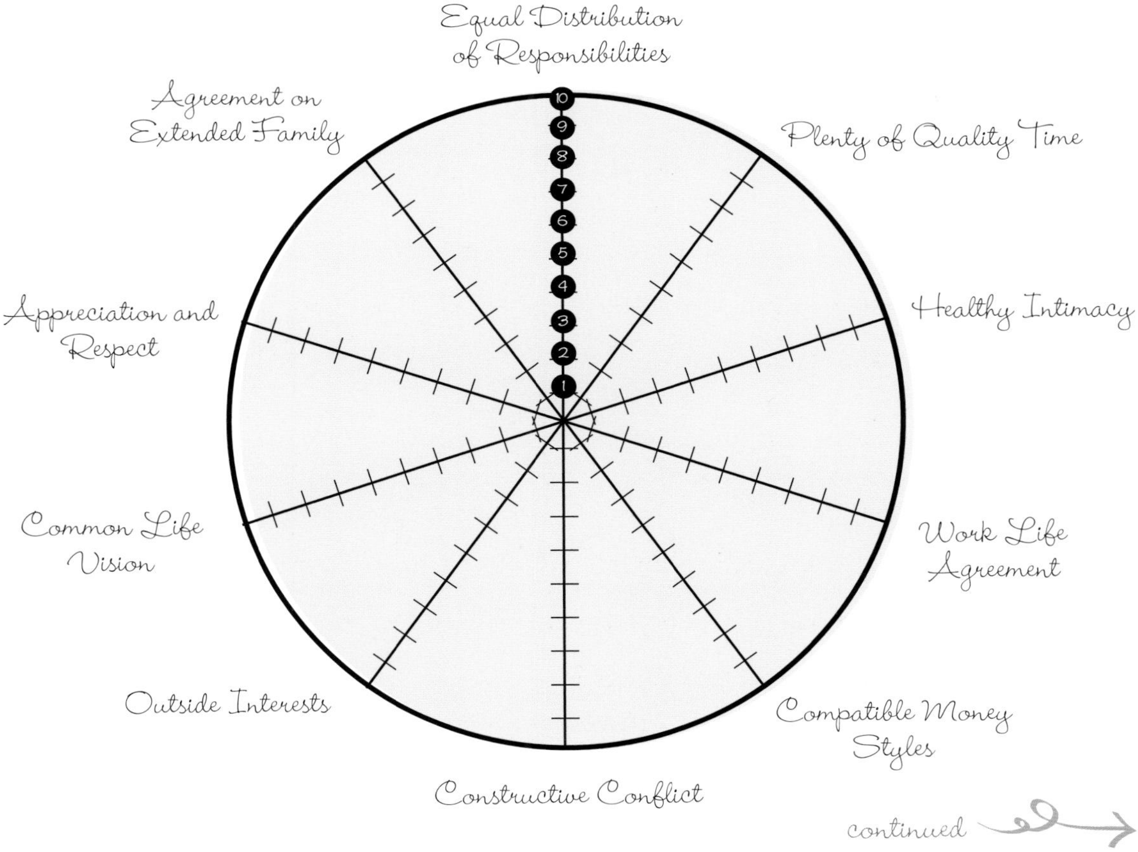

Equal Distribution of Responsibilities

Plenty of Quality Time

Healthy Intimacy

Work Life Agreement

Compatible Money Styles

Constructive Conflict

Outside Interests

Common Life Vision

Appreciation and Respect

Agreement on Extended Family

10 9 8 7 6 5 4 3 2 1

continued

Category	Explanation
Equal distribution of responsibilities	Do you and your partner share responsibilities (cleaning, cooking, pet care, dry cleaning pickup) in a way that feels fair?
Plenty of quality time	Do you make enough time to enjoy each other's company?
Healthy intimacy	Are you and your partner intimate in ways that satisfy both of you?
Work life agreement	Are you and your partner happy with the amount of time and energy you each devote to work?
Compatible money styles	Have you reached agreement about how to handle your money in terms of spending and saving?
Constructive conflict	Do you disagree in constructive rather than destructive ways?
Outside interests	Do you both build connections with other people and have activities beyond your relationship?
Common life vision	Do you agree on major life topics, such as where to live, preferred number of children, how to discipline children, and religious/spiritual practices?
Appreciation and respect	Do you show sufficient appreciation and respect for each other?
Agreement on extended family	Have you reached agreement about how often and when to spend time with extended family?

GETTING ORGANIZED

If you and your partner are planning a wedding without the help of a professional, you can avoid unnecessary stress by getting organized. Need the catering contract to double-check one of the prices? Check! Need one more skein of embroidery thread and want to match the exact color? Check! The goal is to have everything—absolutely everything—related to wedding planning at your fingertips.

Between the office supply store and the Internet, you have great options to choose from when it comes to getting organized. Before you decide on the system that will work best for you, consider the kinds of things you might need to keep track of:

- Everything you'll need to bring to the wedding
- The guest list with addresses
- Receipts
- Contracts with vendors
- Vendors' business cards
- Your ongoing to-do list
- Fabric or ribbon samples
- Presents you receive
- Ideas for registry items
- Jobs to dole out
- Copies of your wedding ceremony program/text and vows

As you can see from this list of sample items, you'll need to corral a mix of hard copies, tangible items, and things that are often stored electronically. You have two primary choices: a paper-based system or a hybrid paper-based and electronic system

For a paper-based system, I recommend a binder with dividers, notebook paper, and pouches. If you are trying to economize, consider making your own dividers out of heavy paper, with sticky notes folded over like tabs and covered in tape to keep them from bending or falling off. Instead of purchasing pouches, you can punch holes in envelopes.

For a hybrid system, I recommend a centralized place that can be accessed via the Internet, so you don't have to have your own computer with you. If you store your documents on the Internet (with something like Google Docs), you and your partner can access the information separately. You might also consider printing your documents and adding the printouts to your binder. That way, you'll have everything in one place and always have it when you need it.

The most important thing is to find a system that works for you. Remember, the goal is to have everything related to your wedding in as few places as possible. You also want your system to be as portable as possible. You might be at a thrift store searching for glass vases and suddenly need to know how many tables are at your reception site.

Regardless of which system you choose, organizing information into categories will help you find what you need, when you need it. Here are some suggested categories for organizing information (but adjust them based on *your* wedding):

- Budget
- Timelines
- Guests
- Ceremony
- Reception
- Attire
- Stationery
- Photography/videography
- Flowers
- Legal
- Miscellaneous

PLANNING THE CALENDAR

There's a lesson to be learned about wedding planning from *Harry Potter*. Instead of getting overwhelmed and giving up when faced with a daunting task (defeating his enemy, Lord Voldemort), Harry tackled the task in smaller pieces (by dealing with the Horcruxes one by one).

In other words, take the potentially daunting prospect of planning a meaningful and memorable event for your nearest and dearest and break it into smaller tasks. Then spread those tasks out over the calendar between now and your wedding. Focus on one thing at a time. This strategy works whether you're getting married in two years (focus on one thing a month) or in two weeks (focus on one thing a day). This strategy also works best if you keep the categories big (attire; catering; music) and give each big category a chunk of time instead of breaking the category down into many small tasks (find a dress; take dress to the seamstress; find shoes; find a hairpiece). You'll eventually need to break the big categories down into specific steps, but now is the time to spread everything out over the entire wedding planning process. And, by the way, if something on the list doesn't get done, your wedding will still go on and you will be married in the end (unless, perhaps, you forget the marriage license!).

"Go confidently in the direction of your dreams. Live the life you have imagined."
—Henry David Thoreau

BUILDING YOUR TO-DO LIST

Once you have a big-picture plan of when you're going to tackle each of the big pieces, break down those pieces even further. Each big chunk (such as the wedding website) will involve several smaller tasks. The more you break down those tasks, the more manageable the work will feel. Writing "Create our wedding website" on your to-do list is a recipe for procrastination and avoidance. That single task is too big and overwhelming. Instead, break it down as far as you can into bite-size action steps. Of course, this process will make your list very long, but each item is likely to feel manageable and increase your motivation to tackle it. Instead of "Create our wedding website," think smaller:

- Search Google for free wedding websites and bookmark the ones you like
- Make a list of features and sections you want the site to contain (such as an online RSVP, "About Us," and "Things to Do")
- Decide which service to use to make the website (for example, mywedding.com or theknot.com)
- Draft text
- Select photos
- Upload photos to the site
- Revise the site
- Publish!

The smaller each task, the more likely you'll be able to complete it in one sitting and check it off. It also helps to use a verb at the beginning of each to-do item. This will help you focus on the action needed. So instead of writing

"What is it you plan to do with your one wild and precious life?"
– poet Mary Oliver

"rings" on your to-do list, for example, write, "Search for rings on Etsy.com." You can make your lists on sheets of paper (one page per category), use a Web application, or use a spreadsheet to list action items, categories, and dates. The exact system you choose is not important. What's important is that you find a system that works for you.

IDEAS FOR NEXT STEPS

- Now is the time to be creative. When you first start the planning process, your options are wide open. The type of wedding you have, the location, the atmosphere—all of it is up in the air. As you progress through the process, your choices will become increasingly limited (because they will all be made within the framework you established at the beginning).
- Use the "Vision Setting Worksheet" to dwell in possibility and imagination. Remember to start with the big picture before thinking through all the smaller details.
- Now is the time to scour the Internet for ideas. Weddings are a popular blog topic, with lots of photos that will surely give you ideas. Indulge in wedding porn (um, that's what the blogging world calls pages and pages of beautiful wedding photography) to your heart's content. Looking at tons of wedding photos might make you question your own choices, so take advantage of the Internet now, before anything is set in stone.
- Make and hang your vision collage. Hopefully, it will help you stay focused on what really matters.

- Talk through the "Wedding Formula Worksheet" with your partner to get a sense of which "traditional" wedding elements you want to retain, reject, revise, or reinvent.
- Come up with the wedding mantras that can help you stay grounded and sane as you embark on your wedding planning journey. Post them where you will see them frequently.
- Enroll in premarital counseling to get your marriage off on the right foot.
- Complete the "Partnership Assessment" to delineate your strengths and areas for growth as a couple.
- Find productive ways to collaborate on wedding planning. Different strategies will work for different couples. Finding ways to deal with conflict and stress is integral to setting yourself up for a successful marriage.
- Create a centralized place to collect everything related to wedding planning.
- Plot the big categories on your calendar, so you have a sense of how and when to fit everything in.
- Break the big categories into specific action steps (with verbs). Keep your to-do list in a centralized place.
- Have fun and remember that there are no rules. In fact, feel free to ignore anything or everything on this list (and every other list) that doesn't resonate with you. Plan the most joyful wedding *for you!*

THE BIG STUFF: Engagement, Budget, Venue, and Guests

Once your wedding vision is in place and you have created a wedding planning process, it's time to get started.

In this chapter, we talk about the benefits and drawbacks associated with shorter and longer engagements. Then we chat about engagement rings. We touch on ways to announce the engagement (with a brief detour about calling off the wedding, if necessary). Then we get into how to make some big decisions, such as who will pay for your wedding, how many people will be invited, what you want to spend your time doing, how much you can afford to spend (with a short discussion about how to combat regional pricing), where to host your ceremony and reception (including a backup location in case it rains), how to pick a day and time, and how to build community among your guests. Finally, we address selecting your officiant and investigating marriage license requirements in your state. By the end of this chapter, you will have put some serious thought into the foundation of your wedding, upon which everything else will be built.

OUR STORY

Matt and I didn't think much about the benefits and drawbacks of a short engagement versus a long one when we decided in December to get married the following July. The length of our engagement was a result of logistics, impatience, and seasonal preference.

At the time, we were both working at public Montessori schools in Denver. Our plan was to move back to Houston by the end of the following summer. We thought getting married in the mountains would be lovely, and we wanted to get married when it was warm outside. So getting married in the mountains of Colorado right before we moved to Houston made the most sense.

We had already lived together for more than a year, so we had adjusted to the idea of a committed, monogamous, lifelong partnership. We opted for a relatively short engagement—seven months—and hunkered down to start the planning.

In addition to an unconventional proposal and an unconventionally short engagement, we also went the unconventional route when it came to an engagement ring: We didn't have one. We opted for a ring-less engagement for a variety of reasons.

On the practical front, I don't typically wear rings, and the thought of wearing two (an engagement ring plus a wedding ring) for the rest of my life was a bit overwhelming. It didn't occur to me at the time that my engagement ring could have become my wedding ring.

On the feminist front, I often wonder why only women walk around with visual evidence that they are engaged. What does this say about the relationship? That men aren't "taken" until the actual ceremony, when they put on a ring too? That the best or only way to show love and commitment is by spending money?

On the historical front, I knew from reading *One Perfect Day* that the notion of a diamond engagement ring (which feels like an indelible part of our culture) is actually a construct of the wedding industrial complex. In the 1930s, a massive advertising campaign was launched to "convince the American consumer that a diamond ring was an indispensable token of romantic love's measure."

On the financial front, the size of a diamond is often seen as a measure of love. Many people buy the biggest diamond they can (or can't) afford. I know a couple who are ready to be married but aren't yet engaged because the man is trying to amass enough funds to surprise his girlfriend with an expensive ring. I can't help but wonder: Shouldn't our commitment determine when we get married, instead of our bank accounts?

On the wedding planning front, we had other details to think through and plans to make, and we needed time to find rings that were environmentally and ethically right for us. My unconventional choice to not wear an engagement ring confused many people, but the decision made sense for me. It was my first important lesson about how to distinguish between what I've been told a wedding is supposed to be and what actually makes sense for my partner and me.

To simplify the early wedding planning stage even further, Matt and I decided to take the easy road when it came to announcing our engagement (which also happened to be a very budget- and eco-friendly road). We called our family and closest friends and e-mailed everyone else (and of course changed our relationship status on various social networking sites). We attached pictures of ourselves dressed up for Halloween (me as a picnic; Matt in a child's dinosaur costume) to the e-mail but decided not to invest too much time and creativity in the process. With the save-the-date notices and formal invitations on the horizon, we figured we would conserve our energy for bigger projects to come.

The one difficult call to make was to Matt's family. Matt's parents are not scary people. In fact, they are wonderful. Matt's mom bought me birthday and Valentine's Day presents as soon as I started dating her son. Matt's dad always sets aside his work at a bank to answer our questions about mortgages and taxes. However, when Matt called to tell them we were engaged, a tingle of uncertainty and anxiety loitered in my stomach. Are we doing the right thing? Am I ready? Seriously, we're getting m-a-r-r-i-e-d?

Upon hearing the announcement, they immediately offered to help with the cost. (See? I told you they're nice.) Matt replied, "No, no, we want to do it ourselves." He explained that a few of our friends had gotten into serious squabbles with their families over wedding plans. He added, "And in those situations, the people paying for it get to decide. We want to have the control."

Ouch.

When he got off the phone, I suggested that we come up with a better PR and marketing plan for this wedding of ours.

It's no wonder that the parental tension started. Matt's mom plans big university events as part of her job and seemed extremely hurt that we were excluding her from the process. She couldn't understand why we didn't want her help. Matt's dad got on the phone and attempted to cajole Matt to be more sensitive to his mom's needs. Even Matt's middle brother, a very laid-back guy who doesn't easily get wrapped up in drama, said, "You better do something to make Mom feel better."

While we didn't want others' financial contributions, we didn't want to alienate family members who wanted to help out with the wedding planning. We realized early on that planning a wedding has different layers of challenges.

Since we had decided to pay for our wedding without any help, we had to determine a budget that meshed with our teacher salaries and allowed us to continue saving for a down payment on our first house, as well as other personal priorities, such as a yearly vacation adventure.

The process for deciding on our $2,000 budget was a very arbitrary one. The gray Saturday morning after our engagement announcement, Matt was flipping through a magazine, showing me pictures of Belize. My mind started to wander to warmer places: "How about a vacation in Belize?" Matt was gloomy: "If we're saving money for a wedding, there's no way we can go to Belize." Then we had an inspiration—why not have a $2,000 wedding? One thousand from each of us. That would surely leave room for a trip to Belize. More importantly, $2,000 seemed like a perfectly reasonable amount to spend on a celebration of love and commitment with our closest friends and family.

And with that, our budget was set. It was a budget that would: (a) keep us out of debt and allow us to save money for a down payment on a house; (b) allow us to pay for the wedding completely on our own (which would help us retain decision-making control, so we could ensure that the wedding represented us and our values); (c) alleviate any guilt we might feel about spending too much money on a one-day celebration; and (d) prevent us from getting sucked into the vortex of the wedding industrial complex.

In a way, Matt and I pulled our $2,000 budget out of thin air. We didn't think through everything we would have to buy for our wedding. We simply came up with a number that seemed reasonable for a weekend celebration. When we actually sat down to create a detailed budget breakdown, I felt my optimism wither. Every category felt tight, with no money left over for a miscellaneous category. Every bridal book I read said we needed to have that category.

Here's what our initial budget looked like:

Sara and Matt's Wedding Budget

Item	Projected Cost	Percent of Budget
Location	$250	13%
Sara's attire	$200	10%
Matt's attire*	$0	0%
Photography	$0	0%
Reception catering	$500	25%
Alcohol/drinks	$450	23%
Decorations/flowers	$50	3%

* Matt wore something he already owned.

Item	Projected Cost	Percent of Budget
Welcome picnic	$200	10%
Invitations	$50	3%
Scrapbook	$50	3%
Marriage license	$10	1%
Music	$0	0%
Cakes	$150	8%
Thank-you cards	$40	2%
Hair and makeup	$0	0%

Figuring out the percentage of the budget for each item helped us keep things in perspective. We wanted to spend the most money on our guests and their enjoyment, so our highest-cost categories were the reception catering and alcohol. I set the budget for my dress high ($200—as much as the entire welcome picnic) because I wanted to find a dress I really liked. I wanted to feel beautiful and confident at our wedding. I felt a little better about that high number because we weren't spending any money on professional hair and makeup, and the $200 included everything associated with my attire—including shoes. Also, my goal was to find a dress that I could wear for years and years. It didn't seem unreasonable to spend $200 on it.

Since we knew that we only had $2,000, we started plugging in different numbers into each category. We created the budget in Excel and used the AutoSum function to calculate how much money had already been allocated. We inevitably went over $2,000 on our first stab at it, so we went back and cut from different areas. For example, the "Decorations/Flowers" category got cut way back, since it seemed least aligned with our goals. It was a "nice-to-have" but not a "need-to-have" category for us.

Having such a relatively modest budget made the prospect of finding a good venue even more daunting. To add to the pressure, we were in a hurry to select a location for the ceremony and reception so we could finalize the date and send out save-the-date messages for out-of-towners who would need time to plan travel.

Matt's mom has excellent research skills, so I asked her to help us find a wedding location. In an attempt to clearly communicate the kind of wedding we wanted to have, I e-mailed her a list of criteria. I wasn't sure what kind of wedding she was imagining. Her own wedding had been on the smaller and more intimate end of the spectrum, but her nephew's wedding just six months earlier had been more like a gala. I tried to be as specific as possible, so the brainstorming list included the following:

- We want to be able to spend quality time with our friends and family, so we would like to rent out an entire B&B, group of cottages, ranch, lodge, etc., to have something more like a family reunion.
- We want everyone to be able to enjoy nature: hiking trails, a campfire, etc. (a lake with canoeing and swimming would be ideal), at a leisurely pace.
- We want to find the right balance between comfortable accommodations and reasonable ones. In other words, we don't want everyone to sleep in bunks, but we also don't want people to have to spend $200-plus per night for a room.
- We are really trying to stay within a $2,000 budget. I know that sounds nearly impossible for a wedding these days, but it's important to us not to spend a lot of money (ours or anyone else's) on one day. We'd rather have the money go toward a honeymoon or a down payment on our first house. If we can find someplace that we can fill up with all our guests (who will pay for their own rooms), then we would probably be able to use a lot of the facilities without having to pay a ton.
- I want to dance outside. I'm not sure if that means a deck or renting a dance floor or what. I just know that I love dancing under the stars.

- In terms of the guest list, we're at a whopping 160 right now! But given the fact that nearly everyone will be traveling from out of town, I'm sure the numbers will dwindle significantly. I also think we could trim the guest list if we found the perfect place that couldn't accommodate that many.

Matt's mom was eager to help, but she wasn't as sold on the $2,000 idea as we were. She expressed her doubts via e-mail:

> *I know you and Matt are worried about keeping your wedding reasonable and I admire that, believe me. But, unfortunately, everything is expensive nowadays. . . . I think you can have a very special day and not spend a fortune but I also think it might be very hard to stick to a $2,000 budget.*

I secretly doubted us too. Everything we came across was wildly expensive, more so if the facility was being used for a wedding. For example, at one of our top contenders, a mountain lodge, we could rent out the meeting room and deck (including tables and folding chairs) for an entire day for a mere $350 for a reunion. If we were throwing a wedding instead of a reunion, however, the exact same space for the exact same number of people would cost $1,800 for five hours, with any additional time at $300 per hour. So the same space for the same amount of time would cost $350 for a reunion and $7,500 for the wedding. To be fair, the wedding price also included "banquet" chairs (instead of regular folding chairs); cake, gift, and guest book tables; tableware; tablecloths; napkins; and a dance floor.

We even thought about tricking the lodge into thinking we were planning a reunion. We had visions of sneaking all our guests to a little corner of the property to witness our stealthy exchange of vows and considered handing out T-shirts that read "Cotner-Bradford Family Reunion" for folks to wear around the lodge. However, being sneaky and dishonest didn't sound like an appealing way to start our new life together.

The only time I ever regretted our relatively short engagement was during the initial process of securing a location. As we scoured the state of Colorado for the ideal location, we quickly learned that Colorado is a popular place to be in the summer and that smart people plan far ahead, getting the best locations and leaving little for the latecomers.

I started reading tips for planning a family reunion, since we wanted more of a family reunion than a traditional wedding, but the advice from the *Colorado Vacation Directory* was downright frightening: "Organizing a family reunion can be a daunting task. How are you going to house, feed and entertain dozens—or even hundreds—of relatives?" Its number-one piece of advice:

Start planning your reunion as early as possible. Most experts recommend at least a year of planning time, but if your reunion will take place at a high-demand location, you might want to start even earlier. At the YMCA of the Rockies in Estes Park, families begin planning reunions an average of two years in advance.

Gulp!

To make matters worse, we were getting familial pressure from both sides during our Christmas vacation: "If you could just tell us the date . . . "

We returned to the idea of the mountain lodge and thought about how to pretend that our wedding was a reunion to make it fit within our budget. We were ready to call and schedule a visit. Unfortunately (which actually turned out to be fortunately), our friend Andy pulled up the location on tripadvisor.com, a site for reviews from travelers, and found these comments: "My aunt had to scrub the bathroom floor and the bathtub before she could let her grandchildren enter"; "For the 21st century it is hard to believe that this kind of accommodation is still on the market." And a short but sweet summary: "I wouldn't stay here if it was the last place in town."

We were back to square one. Again.

We started searching in other states, optimistic that it would be easier to find something that wasn't in a major summer destination state like good ol' Colorado. We quickly realized that it would be too difficult to plan a wedding from afar.

I spent the majority of my Christmas vacation poring over online directories of B&Bs, lodges, cabins, homes for rent, ranches, condos, and even monasteries. I was determined to find something—anything!—that would accomplish our goals. I quickly came to the conclusion that wedding planning wasn't all that fun. I started to resent the fact that I was spending so much time searching for a venue while Matt was spending time relaxing with his family. He just didn't feel the same sense of urgency. My eruption into tears in the middle of the airport on our way back home from our vacation helped him see things from my perspective. Big, fat, rolling tears. I explained—through gulps and gasps—that we didn't have any options. Our wedding was in seven months, and we didn't have a single idea about where to hold it. I was convinced that any place we did find would already be booked.

We went back to our original vision of what we were looking for and decided to start compromising. Maybe we didn't need a space big enough to house everyone. Maybe our closest friends and family could stay on-site with us and other folks could bunk down the road. Then we remembered a little B&B we had stayed at back in September: Sunshine Mountain Lodge. It wasn't big enough to house everyone, but it might be big enough for a ceremony and reception. Surely, there were other lodging options right down the road that could accommodate the rest of the group.

We immediately called to ask about availability for renting the entire site. The place had one weekend left. If a tiny hole-in-the-wall B&B had only one weekend available for the entire month of July, we were in serious trouble. Miraculously, we managed to find one other option: Shadow Mountain Ranch. It, too, had one weekend left for the entire summer.

We left Denver early on a Saturday morning to visit our top two (er, only two) venue options. We headed due west, straight into the mountains.

At Shadow Mountain Ranch, it was difficult to imagine what the winter landscape would look like in summer. Most everything was covered in snow, and the majority of trees were stripped of their leaves. A man named Jim took us for a tour around the grounds. The cabins were just perfect—quaint, with solid wood construction. I could imagine our guests entering their cabins and excitedly settling in for a weekend in the woods. There was even an ideal spot for a ceremony down by the lake, as well as a hot tub!

Jim explained that the lake was right near a building we could use for our reception. The wooden structure reminded me a bit of a frat house, with its musty plaid couch with torn seams, the requisite neon sign, and, of course, lots of empty beer bottles.

I was not going to be dissuaded by a little grime, however. Or even a lot of grime. The truth was that we had only one other venue option, one too small to be truly appealing. I had visions of giving the place a good scrub down, adding some Christmas lights, and bringing in some cleaner chairs.

When we went back to the main lodge to talk through details, we took out our binder with our list of questions and space to write down answers. We had one important question: "When we did an Internet search for your place, we saw that it's for sale."

"Oh yeah, I put it on the market several months ago, and I imagine it will be on the market for a while. It shouldn't be a problem."

Desperately wanting to believe that it wouldn't be a problem, I asked, "So what would happen if we booked the place and then you sold it?"

"Well, I guess you'd have to figure something else out."

Right. Figure something else out. I was already anticipating that we would have lots of bumps and jostles along the wedding planning road, but the last thing we needed was to be forced to find a new venue at the last minute.

It should have been a deal breaker. A nonnegotiable. But we were so desperate for a place that we kept asking questions and diligently taking notes.

After several hours of driving and several stops along the side of the road, we finally pulled into our second option, Sunshine Mountain Lodge. Unfortunately, it was as small as we remembered, and the cabins just as underwhelming. It was situated right on the highway. But Cathy and Cory, the innkeepers, were just as welcoming as we remembered. They gave us a tour and talked about the few weddings they had hosted. They also volunteered to cater our event for $15 per person. It became increasingly clear that the weddings they had hosted were much smaller than we anticipated our wedding would be. I couldn't envision a single spot on their property that would fit all our guests for the ceremony. The only way I could see making the wedding reception work involved setting up tables in the parking lot.

I was completely defeated and deflated. We drove home in grumpy silence. Well, I guess I should say I was grumpy and silent, and Matt decided not to attempt much conversation with me.

I was at the end of my proverbial rope. I honestly couldn't imagine another minute spent searching for a location. I had literally looked at every website of every cabin, lodge, ranch, B&B, hotel, motel, and retreat center within a two-hour radius of the Denver International Airport. My life had quickly become consumed with wedding planning, and I hated it. It was stressful and disappointing and unrewarding. I knew that picking the right location was important; I just couldn't find what we were looking for.

Matt wasn't as worried as I was. He said he was fine having it at Sunshine Mountain Lodge. He felt like there was enough space for a ceremony, and he was okay with the fact that it was situated on a major thoroughfare. I started to worry that our strict budget would hinder the quality of our wedding.

The clock kept ticking, and I became increasingly anxious to settle on a location. Matt and I listed the pros and cons for each location. Shadow Mountain Ranch: beautiful setting, great location for a ceremony, quaint cabins, okay spot for reception, risk of being sold and completely unavailable for our wedding. Sunshine Mountain Lodge: supernice innkeepers, very reasonably priced, not much space, not as aesthetically appealing as Shadow Mountain, located on a highway.

I realized that my tendencies toward perfectionism were making the process very difficult. My rational voice reminded me that I didn't need to find the perfect location. Time for my mantra: A wedding is about commitment, community, connection, and fun. As long as the location fostered those things, smaller details (such as proximity to the highway) weren't important.

In fact, having a wedding at Sunshine Mountain Lodge would help us emphasize all the right things. Cathy and Cory were amazing people: genuine, kind, hardworking, and funny. If we had a wedding at their place, we would build a relationship with them over several months. Plus, if we rented out the entire facility, we would have the freedom to roam the whole property, which would help make the experience feel more comfortable and relaxed.

We went back to our goals:

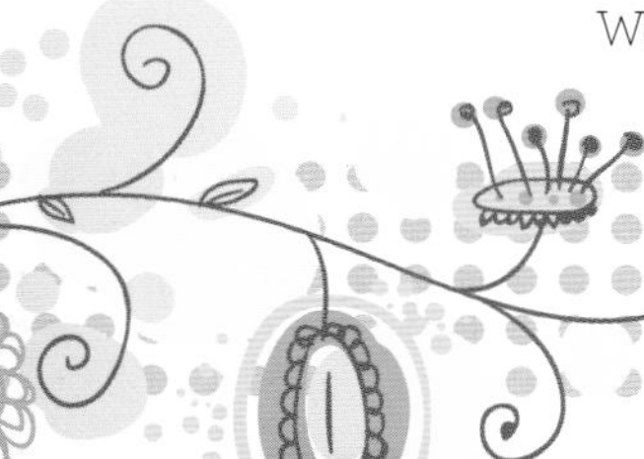

- Would hosting our wedding at Sunshine Mountain Lodge help us bring together family and friends to reconnect and form new friendships? Yes. Friends would be grouped into cabins together. Sharing living space would give them even more opportunities to reconnect.
- Would Sunshine Mountain Lodge keep the experience from feeling overly orchestrated by emphasizing the love aspect of our wedding and not the show aspect? Yes! Sunshine Mountain Lodge has a moose fetish. It has stuffed moose everywhere (the teddy bear, not the taxidermy, kind). It is more on the grandma's house end of the wedding spectrum than the Martha Stewart side.
- Would Sunshine Mountain Lodge help us stay within our budget? Absolutely. We could rent out the entire place (accommodating up to forty people) for a mere $750 per night. If we charged everyone $25 to $35 per person per night, we would have more than enough money.
- Would Sunshine Mountain Lodge be good for the environment and connected to nature? Yes. Cathy and Cory are eco-conscious, and the whole place is smack dab in the middle of a bunch of trees (even though you can still see the highway).
- Would we have real time to spend with our guests? Certainly. We would wake up with them and get to lounge around on the flagstone patio eating the free breakfast.
- Would Sunshine Mountain Lodge help us be relaxed and fully present? Probably. Cathy and Cory seemed eager to help with our wedding. They even seemed genuinely excited about it. Because the place was homey rather than sophisticated, I predicted that the low-key setting would help me feel more relaxed. It would feel more like a family reunion than a performance.

Although I could accept the rather rugged cabin situation at Sunshine Mountain Lodge, could work around the fact that the location would fit only half our guests, could overlook the intermittent noise from passing cars on the highway, and was inspired by how aligned it was with our goals, I couldn't get over the fact that our ceremony would be cramped and not particularly beautiful. Then the idea hit me: Why not look for another location for the ceremony but hold the reception at Sunshine Mountain Lodge?

It's funny how we get locked into certain ways of thinking and lose our ability to think outside the box. I was so intent on having the ceremony and reception in the same location that it took me a long time to realize that there was another way.

Since Sunshine Mountain Lodge would hold only half our guests, I started looking for another B&B that could serve as both an overflow site for the rest of our guests and a beautiful location for our outdoor ceremony. After a bit more Internet searching, I came across Meeker Park Lodge. It looked rustic in a quaint sort of way and seemed to have a beautiful lake with picnic tables. We contemplated having our entire wedding there but learned that we couldn't have alcohol on the premises and would have to end the reception by 10:00 p.m. Since the cabins were a little nicer than the ones at Sunshine Mountain Lodge (and more expensive), it seemed like the perfect place for guests who wanted a more upscale option.

We called to ask how many cabins were available in July and how much it would cost to have our ceremony on site. There were just enough cabins left for the guests who wouldn't fit at Sunshine Mountain Lodge, and the price of using the land as a ceremony site was perfect for our meager budget: free!

We quickly learned that there are benefits to trekking off the beaten path: People are more open to being generous and downright friendly.

Meeker Park Lodge was no wedding factory. We were probably its first wedding. The lodge even agreed to let us use its folding chairs for the ceremony. We just had to be finished with the ceremony by the time the horses were put out to pasture. Without having laid eyes on the actual site, we agreed to a ceremony at Meeker Park Lodge and a reception six miles down the road at Sunshine Mountain Lodge. I figured we could find someplace beautiful to have the ceremony on Meeker's parcel of land. I realized early on that we couldn't blow every detail out of proportion for the next six months.

Looking back on it, selecting the right venues for our ceremony and reception was a linchpin in the whole process. We had found the perfect wedding venue *for us* because we had deprioritized aesthetic considerations and prioritized community and connection. The relationship we were able to forge with the owners of Sunshine Mountain Lodge allowed us to achieve our vision and save a ton of money.

Once we checked off that major item on our wedding to-do list, we turned our attention to other important things, such as how to facilitate community and connection during the wedding weekend. We started by strategizing about how to use our wedding website for that purpose.

First, since many of our guests were flying in from out of town, we created a page devoted to carpooling. On this page, guests could write their arrival and departure times, as well as their e-mail addresses. That way they could connect with people they didn't know to save money and gas.

Second, we installed a widget on our website that allowed guests to upload pictures of themselves with brief bios. The responses were hilarious and fun.

Although only thirty or so guests uploaded their pictures and bios, we enjoyed having this feature on the site.

Because we were bringing together many different groups, we wanted to find as many ways as possible to foster connections. That's why Matt and I created the "Ask me about . . ." name tags. We figured the name tags would facilitate conversation beyond small talk.

To minimize the cost associated with creating name tags, we decided to use paper we already had, even though it happened to be bright orange. I had to remind myself that building community, connection, and fun (and saving money) was more important than aesthetics. Of course, those things don't have to be mutually exclusive, but with our budget they sometimes were.

Luckily, we had a small laminating machine at home (it comes in handy when you teach elementary school), so we printed the name tags on our black-and-white printer and ran them through the laminating machine. Then we used a craft knife to cut small openings at the top of each tag, and we slipped in clips that we purchased on sale from OfficeMax. In total, the project cost $24.

In the end, the bright orange worked out beautifully. It was easy to spot the name tags and to strike up conversations. People were eager to read each other's tags.

During this phase in our wedding planning process, we also had to figure out who was going to officiate our ceremony. We decided against a representative of a church because we have both moved away from our religious roots over the years—me from Presbyterianism and Matt from Catholicism. Although our families would both have preferred a religious officiant, it wasn't something we were willing to compromise on. Matt and I wanted someone who was close to both of us, as well as someone who would be willing to present a ceremony that we wrote. We wanted a strong public speaker who would engage the audience and would calm and comfort us as we proclaimed our commitment to each other. We were also looking for someone who would make us laugh.

The clear choice became my best friend, Andy. Andy is a professor by day and a writer and reality TV expert by night. Over the years, he and Matt have become close friends too. Fortunately, the opportunity to officiate our ceremony excited Andy. He quickly jumped at the chance to become ordained online by the Universal Life Church—even though the state of Colorado did not require such documentation. Although Andy is not the type to squeal with delight, his voice became increasingly animated when he recounted all the new titles he could put in front of his name thanks to his ordination: Reverend Father, Right Reverend, Absolute Reality, Apostle of Humility, Spiritual Warrior, Peace Counselor, Life Facilitator, Soul Therapist, Revelator; the list goes on.

Once we had the ceremony and reception venues chosen, a plan for facilitating community, and our officiant situation worked out, we decided to skip some common elements of the wedding planning process, including engagement photos and parties. Since we had only seven months, we worried that we would get frazzled by cramming in too much. We wanted to streamline the process and conserve energy for everything else on our to-do list.

Once we had the big pieces in place—the budget and the venue—we felt much more settled and optimistic that we might actually pull this thing off.

ENGAGEMENT LENGTH

There's a lot of debate out in the wide wedding world about the ideal length of an engagement. An engagement is not just a transition period from dating to married life; it's also the much-heralded wedding planning period.

On one side, you've got the longer-is-better advocates. They argue:

- The longer you plan your wedding, the more relaxed the process will be.
- You'll have time to search for the best vendors and the best accoutrements.
- You'll get better deals and avoid much of the anxiety associated with the wedding planning process.
- It takes time to settle into the idea of marriage. You need the transition period to fully realize the gravity of your choice, embrace it, and prepare for it.

On the other side, you have the shorter-is-better supporters. They argue:

- The longer you plan your wedding, the more you obsess about details, the more you second-guess your decisions, the more you covet other people's choices, the more your wedding has the potential to overshadow your relationship, the more your life becomes consumed by The Big Day, and the more you lose yourself and find Bridezilla.
- People can pull together funerals and birthday parties in a matter of days—why should a wedding take more than a year?

If you and your fiancé are able to choose the length of your engagement, it's worth considering both perspectives. Will a longer engagement allow you to have a more relaxed planning period, or will you grow tired of wedding planning and find yourselves wishing that the wedding would just hurry up and get here?

To figure out what makes the most sense for you and your partner, talk to your friends and family members who have planned weddings. Ask questions such as:

- How long was your engagement?
- Do you wish it had been longer or shorter, or was it just right?
- What do you see as the benefits and drawbacks of a shorter engagement?
- What do you see as the benefits and drawbacks of a longer engagement?

Be sure to ask the necessary follow-up question: "Why?" Pay attention to different people's rationales and determine what resonates with you.

Rachel and Greg knew they wanted to get married in their favorite season, fall, which gave them a yearlong engagement. Rachel said, "I think I'd have a shorter engagement if I had a do-over because I got ants in my pants and wanted to get my married on!" Camyl and Ryan opted for a much longer engagement—more than two years. Camyl said, "When we got engaged last year, we felt we weren't yet financially ready to have a wedding, much less get married. Ryan had just closed his restaurant business, so he had a lot of financial obligations at that time. So we went for 2010, which seemed like a good year and gave us more than enough time to save up for the wedding. . . . I wouldn't have had it any other way. I had enough time to iron out issues (family as well as relationship issues) and map out our preferences (for the wedding, for the marriage, etc). It's given us so much time to think about the serious things too . . . without feeling like we're in a hurry. The relaxed pace doesn't put so much pressure on us and has made transitioning into married life seem so much easier."

Our seven-month engagement had its benefits and drawbacks. We wouldn't have been able to secure the reception location if we had waited any longer (Colorado plus summer equals hugely popular wedding destination). On the other hand, although we appreciated having plenty of time to undertake lots of DIY projects, we got tired of talking and thinking about our wedding all the time, and we also had leeway to procrastinate. We dragged our feet unnecessarily on a number of decisions (like what kind of beer to purchase).

I wish I could tell you that there's a one-size-fits-all magic length, but there isn't. Every couple must decide for themselves what makes sense. It's true for deciding on the length of your engagement just as it's true for every other aspect of your wedding: Do what feels right for you.

ENGAGEMENT RINGS

When you tell someone you're engaged, the first response is usually, "Ooh! Let me see the ring!" Many of our ideas about weddings start with the engagement ring. If a ring is the way you want to start your engagement, go for it. But know that different people make different and valid choices for themselves, based on who they are as a couple. Other options might include:

- Both partners wear engagement rings.
- Both partners wear their wedding rings as engagement rings.
- Both partners wear their wedding rings on their right hands until the wedding and then switch them to their left hands (as they do in Brazil).
- Partners exchange non-jewelry gifts to symbolize their commitment.
- Neither partner wears an engagement ring.

We all need to decide for ourselves how we want our engagements and weddings to go, regardless of what already feels set in stone (pun intended) by society. Ring or no ring? Diamond or amethyst? Metal or wood? Candy Ring Pop? The choice is yours.

It can be hard to go your own way during this process. It's an emotional time. What you really want is support and encouragement, yet so many people offer up judgment and discouragement. People have all sorts of strong ideas about how a wedding should be (both on the traditional and nontraditional sides). When they find out you're not conforming to their vision, they can make you feel insecure about your choices.

Anne—a bride from Australia—talks about "the blank and puzzled looks of people who couldn't quite comprehend answers to questions like 'What are your bridesmaids wearing?' that involve, 'Um, we're not having bridesmaids.' Or flowers. Or a photographer. Or a bridal party. Or place cards. Or cars. Or colors. We are having a nice dinner at a local restaurant. For thirty people."

During my engagement, I faced similar reactions whenever I revealed some of our unconventional wedding choices. For example, I attended a wedding and started talking to a cousin of the bride. When she found out I was engaged, she said, "Oh, give me your hand!" Naively, I thought that she literally wanted to hold my hands, maybe as a show of support, and I placed both my hands in hers. Confused—both by the fact that I had put two hands in hers and by the fact that I wasn't wearing a ring—she said, "Oh, where's your ring?"

Facing others' assumptions, questions, and explicit judgments (as well as implicit judgments) can make you want to cry, scream "Back off," or elope. I had to keep reminding myself of this wedding mantra: "Those who mind don't matter, and those who matter don't mind." It can be helpful to return to this idea throughout the wedding planning process to stay on the path that makes sense for you and your partner.

ANNOUNCING THE ENGAGEMENT

Right before Matt and I got engaged, we received an engagement announcement in the mail from our friends Camella and Kevin. It featured a photo of the happy couple in a gorilla costume and a French maid's outfit—with an accordion. The postcard read, "We don't yet know where or when, but we know to whom."

Announcing your engagement can be as basic or as creative as you want. After considering all the options, decide what makes the most sense for you. Options include:

- Letting the word spread organically by calling family, updating social media networks, and telling people in person
- Mailing announcements
- Making a video, creating a website, or sending out a photo

Give some thought to who will receive the information and when. Family members might be upset to learn about your engagement from their eleven year-old son who sees it on Facebook. Ultimately, announce your engagement in ways that make sense to you, but if you can avoid drama early in the process by making a few adjustments, it might be worth it.

CALLING OFF THE WEDDING

Sometimes, in the midst of planning your wedding, you realize you need to cancel it. This section is here to say: If you need to call off your wedding, by all means do it.

Canceling a wedding—no matter how hard it is—is easier than canceling a marriage. So if this section is resonating with that little voice inside your head that's telling you not to go through with it, know that the best thing you can do for yourself and your significant other is to be your authentic self, which includes not getting married to the wrong person for you.

If you have any doubts about going through with the wedding, pay attention to them. If you decide to call it off or even just postpone the wedding, use the organization system you've created to figure out whom to contact, what paperwork needs to be done, and what refunds and costs may be involved. Get help from close friends and family, and be kind to yourself.

If you broadcast your engagement to wide circles, be prepared for some people to mistakenly assume that they will be invited to the wedding. Consider preparing a response, such as, "We won't be able to create the guest list until we've finalized the venue."

WHO FOOTS THE BILL?

One thing I learned from years of slumber parties at my friends' houses during elementary, middle, and high school was that families are, well, different. Families who eat vastly different foods, have different rules related to R-rated movies, and have different bedtimes for their kids also do weddings differently.

I have a couple of friends whose families said things along the lines of, "We're going to give you $30,000. You can use as much or as little of it as you want for your wedding. The rest can go toward a down payment on your first house. No strings attached." And they meant it. On the other hand, I know people who received "no strings attached" money from their families and ended up regretting it. "No strings attached" became, "Of course we will have a sit-down dinner. I did not give you money for your wedding so you could go spend it on a taco truck."

When deciding whether or not to use family money to subsidize your wedding, the trick is to "know thyself and thy family" (then add a little bit of caution, in case they unsuspectingly morph into Familyzilla). Think about your style and your preferences. Do they align with your family's style and preferences? Are your visions of a good time similar? How controlling have your family members been in the past? Do they worry about how things look to their friends?

It's possible to accept money from your family and still have a wedding that represents you and your fiancé. Or you may consciously decide that you want your wedding to represent your whole family, so you're willing to make compromises.

In the end, you have to remember that money is power. Your family members may not choose to exert power over you if you accept their money, but they can if they want to. If you want to accept their money (because you need it to have the kind of wedding you want; because you want a wedding that reflects your family as well as you and your fiancé), remember that you may lose some of your decision-making power. Think through all the options (and the potential consequences) before making your choice.

As with all wedding-related decisions, you and you partner have to do what feels right to you. No one but you can make this decision. Take time to think through your various choices and keep in mind all the potential ramifications of each choice. A good question that will help you process each option is, "What's the worst that could happen if __________?"

Ways to Foot the Bill

Option	Pros	Cons
Pay for the whole wedding yourselves	You can ensure that the wedding completely reflects the values of you and your fiancé. You will have a sense of accomplishment that comes from being self-sufficient as a couple. You will have ground to stand on during squabbles with family members.	You may not have enough money to have the kind of wedding you want. If you spend your money on your wedding, you will have less money for other things (home, car, vacation). Your family may feel alienated that you didn't want their support.
Accept money from family	You will have more money to spend on your wedding. You will have more money to spend on other things (home, car, vacation). Your families will feel more involved in the wedding planning process, and the wedding will feel like a family effort.	The wedding may reflect your family more than it reflects you and your fiancé. You are more likely to get into squabbles with your family about various elements of the wedding. In the end, the person who pays usually makes the final decision.
Accept money only for specific aspects of the wedding	By turning over certain aspects (for example, alcohol or flowers) to your family, you can have more money to spend while retaining control over aspects that are most important to you.	If your families' tastes and preferences are wildly different from your own, your wedding may feel incongruent.
Set out to pay for the wedding yourselves but let your family know you may need help later on	By asking your family to pay for certain things once they have already been decided, you ensure that the wedding completely reflects your values and those of your fiancé. You will have more money to spend as you see fit. You will potentially have fewer squabbles with family members.	Your family might feel slighted by you for not being invited to participate from the beginning. Your family might not want to pay for things without being part of the initial decision-making process.

THE GUEST LIST

The venue determines the tone and overall feeling of your wedding, but so does the size of the guest list. Our list started out gigantic (especially for a $2,000 wedding) at 160. We decided to go at it with a machete because of goal number one for our ideal wedding: "We want to have real time to spend with guests. We want to spend quality time with friends and family. We want more of a family and friends reunion." We knew that the bigger our wedding got, the less opportunity we would have to genuinely connect with our guests. We also didn't want our wedding to feel like a show. We didn't want to feel like celebrities who floated around the room, distanced from the audience. For us, we felt like the bigger our wedding got, the more we would feel like this.

Keeping the list on the short side definitely posed challenges. First, we have a long list of acquaintances. Matt has friends going all the way back to elementary school (so sweet!), and I've accumulated friends through working at Space Camp, doing AmeriCorps, and attending a seminar on utopian studies sponsored by the National Endowment for the Humanities. Second, we're generally nice, nonconfrontational people. Not inviting people to a wedding kind of felt like ringing their doorbells and throwing a bucket of ice water in their faces.

We had to look at the wedding guest list through an honest lens. Some of our strategies included:

- Not feeling obligated to reciprocate invitations. I had people on the list who were there only because I had been invited to their weddings (even though we weren't close friends). I cut those people from the list.
- Being honest. I also had people on the list with whom we wanted to be closer friends. We just weren't. Those people got cut too.
- Not being pressured. Finally, we had listed colleagues whom we felt obligated to invite. We applied the following litmus test: When we move on to our next jobs, will we still be friends with this person? If the answer was no, that person was off the list too.

Of course, this process was easier said than done. My boss and several colleagues assumed they were invited. I had to apologize and explain, "It's a very small wedding. We are able to invite only our closest family and friends."

Luckily, we had the primary say over our guest list because we paid for the wedding ourselves. Of course we consulted with our families and made a few adjustments, but we made sure we would be surrounded by only our closest friends and family (none of our dads' golf buddies, for example, or family friends we hadn't seen in ten years).

If family members pressure you to edit the guest list in ways you disagree with, consider these strategies:

- Be honest and open about the kind of wedding you want and how a certain-sized guest list will help you achieve your vision.
- Remind them that this is your wedding and should reflect you and your fiancé. If they are married, remind them that they already had *their* wedding. (Be sure to say this in a kind and empathetic way!)
- Let your family host a separate reception to which they can invite whomever they want.
- Give your family a limited number of guest slots to fill however they choose. Let them make the tough decisions about which family and friends make the cut.

For us, restricting our guest list to our nearest and dearest was an important part of keeping our wedding focused on community and connection. It was also an important part of staying relaxed and fully present in the moment. We imagined that the more people who attended, the more anxious we would feel about getting a chance to see all of them. Different size guest lists make sense for different couples. The trick is to figure out what kind of wedding you want and to match the guest list to that vision.

THE WEDDING AGENDA

When planning a wedding, people typically spend a lot of time thinking through the details of how guests will spend their time during the reception. Those going the traditional route think about things like: What time will dinner start? When will dancing start? When will "the exit" take place?

Although thinking through an agenda for the ceremony and reception is important, you also need to think about how to spend your nonceremony and nonreception time. You need to look at a wedding as a complete experience, not just a ceremony and reception. How do you want to spend your time leading up to the wedding? Do you want to spend a day getting pampered with your closest friends? Do you want to go on a long private hike with your partner? Do you want to spend the day hanging out with your family? Do you want to have your wedding in the morning so you can relax with your friends for the rest of the day? Do you want to have several events spread out over a couple of days? Do you want your closest friends to arrive early? Do you want to be alone? Do you want to have fun activities, like those listed on the following page?

Ways to Have Fun at Your Wedding

- Cooking s'mores around a campfire
- Soaking in a hot tub
- Playing volleyball
- Playing board games or kid's games (Scrabble, Chutes and Ladders)
- Playing lawn games (bocce ball, croquet, badminton, horseshoes)
- Jumping on pogo sticks
- Having a hula hoop contest, potato sack race, or beanbag toss
- Doing a scavenger hunt
- Playing bingo
- Hosting a talent show
- Hiring a fortune teller or palm reader
- Playing schoolyard games (tetherball, kickball, dodge ball, hopscotch, four square)
- Playing ping-pong or pool
- Making big bubbles
- Playing card games
- Playing Frisbee golf
- Playing charades or Pictionary
- Renting an air hockey table
- Offering chair massages
- Busting open a piñata
- Eating fondue
- Making crafts at a craft table
- Renting a jukebox
- Having a casino night
- Playing with sidewalk chalk
- Adding to a graffiti wall
- Coloring with crayons on tables covered with butcher paper
- Hosting a parade
- Playing video games
- Jumping on a trampoline
- Tailgating and going to a ball game
- Hanging out around a pool
- Attending a wine tasting
- Running around a children's museum
- Looking at art in a gallery
- Painting pottery
- Cruising around a lake or an ocean
- Picnicking
- Hiring an artist to draw caricatures of your guests
- Offering dance lessons (swing, Polynesian, contra, Latin)

The possibilities are almost endless. Think through options and figure out what makes the most sense for you. Once you've made your decisions, you might find that you have to fight to stick to them. Demands can appear out of nowhere like barrels in Donkey Kong. They might come from the photographer, your future mother-in-law, or the maid of honor. If you know what you want, it will be easier to dodge the demands.

BUDGET

Deciding on a budget is a personal process that can vary from couple to couple. Victoria and Joe got married in Washington, D.C., in May and "didn't want to be ascetic" about their wedding; they wanted it to be "joyful and celebratory." They also wanted their "guests to feel loved and taken care of (through good food and little details like sunscreen, bug spray, a tent to shield from sun, etc.)." On the other hand, they "felt that extravagance would be self-centered and socially unjust." Ultimately, they decided on a $5,000 budget because it "felt like a good middle road" for them.

Another couple, Barbara and David, decided on a $3,500 budget. Barbara explained, "We wanted a budget that allowed us to spoil ourselves and our guests a little bit, to continue having a savings account, and that kept us thinking about the wedding as the BEGINNING of our journey together, not the destination."

Megan and Peter opted for a $10,000 budget. Megan said, "It just seemed like that was what it would cost when we sat down to decide what we wanted and what was most important to us."

There's no one-size-fits-all answer to the question of what your wedding budget should be. Further, a budget doesn't have to be set in stone; it can be changed during the planning process. Think of your budget as a compass or a guidepost along the wedding planning journey.

Here are a few pointers for developing your wedding budget:

DECIDE WHAT YOUR OVERARCHING BUDGET IS

People often assume they should spend as much as they can afford to on a wedding, but don't leap to that conclusion. You and your partner should ask yourselves: How much can we spend on our wedding without going into debt or compromising our other financial goals? How much do we want to spend on our wedding? A wedding is both a once-in-a-lifetime event and a one-day party. Settle on a budget that strikes the right balance for you and your fiancé and know that the number is different for every couple.

DELINEATE YOUR CATEGORIES

Wedding books and websites can be helpful for creating a thorough list of categories, but they can also be overwhelming. The list seems to go on forever! As you look at other people's categories, remember that a wedding doesn't have to follow a specific formula. You can eliminate categories altogether or generate new and unique ones.

PLAY WITH THE NUMBERS

If you think about your first budget as a rough draft, it's much less daunting. Excel is an easy tool for this, especially if you use the AutoSum function to add up all your categories. Just plug in some numbers and continue tinkering until the total works out. As you start paying for wedding-related things, continue to play with the numbers. For example, if you go under budget in one category, go ahead and add the extra to another category. Vice versa if you spend too much in a particular category; subtract that amount from other categories. That way, you can reward yourself for coming in under budget and be conscious of how splurges affect your entire budget.

GROUND YOURSELF WITH THE PERCENTAGES

Sometimes dollar amounts can be deceiving. It helps to add a percentage category to get a different perspective. Percentages can help you more easily see where your priorities are.

WEDDING DEBT

For couples under the age of thirty, debt from their wedding is the most common and intense source of conflict, according to a Creighton University study. Among couples of all ages surveyed, wedding debt was the third most troubling issue in their marriage, behind time management and sexual issues.

To avoid these common wedding mistakes, keep the wedding meaningful and manageable. Set aside some of the money you save for a great honeymoon or maybe a house or a baby. And don't forget—enjoy the day.

– Lilo and Gerard Leeds, *Wonderful Marriage: A Guide to Building a Great Relationship that Will Last*

FIGURE OUT THE COST PER GUEST

When you come up with a tentative budget number, do a little calculation to figure out how much you would be spending for each guest. Does it seem too high? Too low? Not every cost in the budget goes toward the guest experience, but this exercise can give you a good perspective.

Of course, you could do what Andrea and her partner did: "We didn't really have a concrete budget; we sort of just started gathering needed items ahead of time and lining up the details." Every couple's situation is very different. We have different incomes, saving habits, families, financial goals, and costs of living. The best we can do is settle on a budget that sits well with us.

REGIONAL PRICING

There's a lot of talk in the bridal blogosphere about regional pricing. It's easy for urban brides to bemoan the inevitably higher costs for venues and vendors in cities that have higher costs of living or seem to attract wedding-planning couples.

To keep expenses reasonable—despite regional pricing—try these tips:

- If you live in an expensive wedding destination, start your venue search just slightly outside of town. You'll probably be able to find something within a reasonable commuting distance that fits your budget.
- Instead of starting with seasoned professionals for things like photography, look toward new professionals who are trying to build their portfolios. You can get an amazing product for a much lower price.
- Avoid all-inclusive "wedding factories" whenever possible. You're more likely to pay an artificially inflated price to businesses that target brides and grooms.

CEREMONY AND RECEPTION VENUES

Once you figure out where to look, you have to figure out what you're looking for. Part of the stress related to finding a location is the realization that the venue is like the first domino. Once it's knocked down, it sets off a chain reaction. For example, the venue determines:

- Your catering options. Some venues don't allow outside catering. Other locations have strict rules about alcohol.
- What kind of decoration is needed. You might feel more pressure to decorate plain spaces.
- What needs to be rented. Some sites come with tables and chairs while others do not.

- The formality of the event. A more relaxed venue creates a more relaxed event. A more sophisticated venue creates a different aesthetic and might make you feel like you have to choose more sophisticated attire or expensive decorations.

Selecting the right venue is challenging for a lot of couples. Maureen and Dave, transplants to the San Francisco area, were in love with the Wine Country but realized that a wedding at a winery was beyond their budget. Most of the wineries they looked at "had ridiculous packages" that locked them into "a certain caterer, a certain deejay, renting tables, having a sit-down ceremony, etc." Maureen said, "When it came right down to it, we just wanted far more control over our wedding than any of these places were willing to give us."

They looked at lodges, inns, beaches, state parks, and even private homes. They decided that "the most important part" was to get their "family and friends together in a place where everyone would be comfortable and have fun." They finally stumbled upon a "restaurant with a large outdoor patio at a really reasonable price." The patio was adjacent to a creek and "shaded by beautiful old trees and landscaped with loads of flowers," so they didn't have to do anything to decorate. The space rental for five hours was $800 and included all the tables, chairs, and linens. Maureen said, "It worked out perfectly because we got the ease of having someone else do the food, setup, and cleanup, but we were able to customize everything else."

One challenge you may encounter is that the location is usually one of the first decisions to be made, early in the process, before you've had a chance to think through your entire wedding. This is one reason creating your wedding vision before you start planning can be helpful.

SELECTING A DATE AND TIME

You'll notice throughout the book that I frequently advise: Don't spend too much time worrying about it; it's not that important. But selecting the right day and time is actually really important. There are many factors to consider, such as:

- What kind of wedding do you want? Do you want a calm, dignified, morning brunch or a raucous dance party that gyrates late into the night?
- If your wedding were on a holiday weekend, would your friends and family appreciate the extra day for traveling or would they have conflicting plans?

- Are the potential savings of hosting your wedding on a nonconventional day and time (such as a Thursday evening or a Sunday) worth the potential inconvenience to guests?
- Do you want to save money by tying the knot in between meals, so you can serve something simple and inexpensive, such as hors d'oeuvres or cake and punch?
- What are the average weather patterns like at that time of year? The online *Old Farmer's Almanac* can be a useful place to look.
- Will anything else influence your decision, such as the moon cycle, honeymoon plans, whether you and your partner are at your best in the morning or later in the day, whether you are more comfortable in warm or cold weather, or even which flowers will be in season?

Once you have a few dates in mind, the next step is to cross your fingers and talk to your desired venue to see which dates are available. The earlier you do this, the better. Many venues fill up quickly and far ahead of time. You'll have more luck if you've selected a quirky venue that doesn't typically host weddings.

Finally, take your list to those family members and friends whom you absolutely want to attend to check their availability and conflicts.

RAIN LOCATION

You can control many things about your wedding day. Unfortunately, weather is not one of them. You can control your response to the weather, however. To maintain your sanity in the days leading up to your wedding, it helps to have a plan about how to deal with inclement weather, especially if you're having an outdoor wedding. (Ask the venue if it has contingency plans for poor weather.) Approaches you can take include:

- Securing a rain location. If rain would have a seriously negative impact on your wedding, you can proactively arrange for a rain location.
- Asking guests to bring umbrellas. If your ceremony is outside, don't rule out simply asking guests to show up with umbrellas (and perhaps providing a few extra for those who forget).
- Booking backup rentals (as long as they can be cancelled). You might be able to rent a tent and cancel it as soon as you know you're in the clear weather-wise. If you go this route, be sure to read the fine print on your contract.

Regardless of which route you take, be confident that bad weather is not likely to ruin your wedding. It may require some last-minute adjustments, affect your plans, or cause bad hair days, but it will not change the love between you and your partner. Nor will it change the fact that your nearest and dearest are happy to be celebrating with you. If anything, it will give you a truly memorable wedding with lots of great stories!

Case in point: On the day of Sarah and Adam's outdoor ceremony, "the forecast improved slightly so that there was only an 80 percent chance of rain for the morning." Committed to having the ceremony outside, they decided to "hope for the best." Thirty minutes prior to the ceremony, it began to rain, but Sarah "surprisingly felt at ease." She said, "I was still getting ready at my parents' house, and nothing could have kept me from smiling."

BUILDING COMMUNITY AMONG GUESTS

Many personal details we think about during wedding planning (hair, makeup, attire) do not impact the guests much, or at all. Instead, our guests are much more likely to enjoy themselves if they feel connected to other people.

One idea for helping your guests feel more connected to each other is to be strategic with the guest list. For example, if you want to invite a colleague from work, consider inviting a second colleague, so that the first has someone to talk to besides his or her plus-one guest. If you go this route, take the extra step to communicate to your guests whom they might know at the wedding. I sent an e-mail to each group of friends (colleagues from my first teaching job, college friends, and so on), letting them know who else from their circle was invited. That way, they didn't have to go around asking everyone we know in common, "Were you invited to Sara's wedding?" It also allowed them to coordinate housing, carpooling, and so forth.

In addition to helping guests connect with people they already know, you and your partner might want to help facilitate new connections among guests, especially if you're bringing together lots of friends and family who don't know each other.

Autumn and her partner took a low-key route. They made name tags for each guest that included the person's relationship to the bride and groom. They hosted a barbecue the night before their wedding to give guests time to mingle.

Fostering community among guests can get quirky and creative. Allison, a master's student from California, and her partner made a crossword puzzle where all the clues had to do with their relationship history. They put it on a big chalkboard and invited guests to solve it together. Although the activity appealed more to their friends than family, it helped friends from each side get to know each other, even if it was, as Allison explained, through "joking and laughing about how ridiculous we were for making a crossword puzzle!"

Other fun ways to build community include:

- Get-to-know-you bingo. This classic team-building icebreaker is great fun at a wedding. Create a bingo grid and fill in each box with a phrase such as "speaks more than two languages fluently" or "knows how to juggle." Everyone has to find someone who fits the criteria and write that person's name in the box. When they've filled in names in a row horizontally, vertically, or diagonally, they can declare "bingo" and win a prize. To encourage more mingling, require that people seek out those they don't know and that they must fill in all the boxes to score a bingo.
- Scavenger hunts. The possibilities and variations are endless. For example, you could ask tables to work together to take pictures of all sorts of things, such as "someone doing rabbit ears above the groom's head" or "the whole table posing like Charlie's Angels."
- Board games. If you go this route, consider recruiting friends or family members ahead of time to be in charge of encouraging people to play.

Keep in mind more subtle opportunities for building community, such as hosting a casual event the day before or after your wedding, asking friends and family from various circles to help out with different parts of the preparation, or intentionally introducing guests you think might get along well.

Regardless of what ideas you come up with, it's best to make them optional. Some guests may not be comfortable with activities and would prefer to chat with people they already know. Don't take it personally; allow for it.

THE OFFICIANT AND MARRIAGE LICENSE

The officiant (or lack thereof) sets the tone for the entire ceremony—that is, the formal exchange of vows and public declaration of intent and commitment. For some people, deciding on the person to lead the ceremony is easy. They choose a pastor from their family church whom they've known for years, or a family member who happens to be a justice of the peace.

Close friends of ours—Loren and Lisa—chose not to have an officiant at all. Lisa's sister escorted them down the aisle, said a few words to open the ceremony, and then joined the audience. For the rest of the ceremony, the couple spoke to each other about why they loved each other and what they promised to each other. It was the most sincere and touching ceremony I have ever witnessed.

Our friends Camella and KT originally wanted to go with a friend as an officiant but were pressured by family to go with a religious figure. They compromised by inviting a friend to officiate who was spiritual in his beliefs, although he did not belong to an organized religion.

As you think through your officiant decision, these questions might be of help:

- To what extent do you want to write your own ceremony? Will the officiant be comfortable with your preferences?
- Will your officiant make time to meet with you as often as needed to create and finalize the ceremony?
- How comfortable do you feel around your officiant? Does his or her presence calm you?
- Will the officiant's personality set the right tone for your wedding ceremony?
- What are the legal requirements of your state?

Doing a quick Google search for "marriage laws by state" can give you the information you need to understand all your options. Investigate your state's requirements sooner rather than later, since waiting periods or specific time frames might be in place.

Those who want the officiant to be a friend or family member but whose state doesn't accommodate this arrangement can get legally married at a courthouse and then have a separate wedding ceremony in front of family and friends with the officiant of their choice. Plenty of couples get legally married before their actual weddings for insurance or other reasons. Most of them report that their weddings were still significant and profound, even though they were technically married already.

IDEAS FOR NEXT STEPS

- Figure out an engagement length that makes sense for you.
- Decide what to do about engagement rings. Figure out where your values, budget, lifestyle, and aesthetics intersect.
- Announce your engagement as simply or as creatively as you want. Remember to conserve energy (and funds) for other to-do items on the horizon.
- Create a guest list that reflects the people you want to celebrate your wedding with.
- Draft your wedding agenda to get a sense of how you want to spend your time before and after the wedding. The in-between times matter too.

- Create your working budget early in the process.
- Pick a couple of wedding dates and send them around to people you absolutely would not want to miss your wedding.
- When you book venues and vendors, get everything in writing. Verbal communication is sometimes like a game of telephone; miscommunication is commonplace. Getting everything in writing is good for contractual purposes and for holding people accountable for what they said they would do; it also helps clarify both parties' understanding of the situation. Maybe you heard the vendor say that she would set up the folding chairs, but she thinks you are going to set them up. Taking the time to nail down all the details up front will save you a lot of hassle and stress later on (especially on your wedding day). This process can be as simple as sending a follow-up e-mail that says, "This is what I understand from our conversation . . ."
- Select your officiant based on the tone you want for your ceremony. Meet with your officiant leading up to the wedding.
- Investigate the marriage license process in your state.
- Have fun!

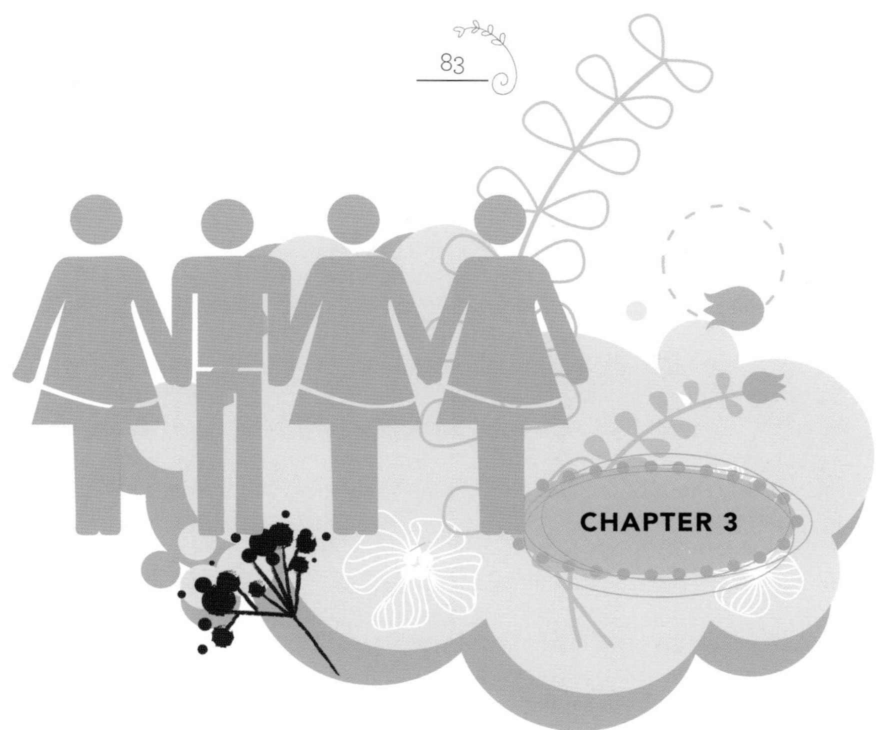

GETTING THE BALL ROLLING: Your Team and Wedding Communications

Once the major decisions are made and the framework is in place, we move into the next stage of planning, which involves selecting your wedding party, deciding how much help you want and from whom, and getting over the guilt of asking for help.

Then we transition into sharing information with your guests, such as designing a wedding website, creating save-the-date notices, sending invitations, and setting up a registry. We also touch on wedding showers. This chapter includes two ideas for DIY projects: a simple, budget-friendly invitation, and a rubber stamp for personalizing your wedding stationery. This section starts with Matt's and my story and ends with specific ideas for your next steps.

OUR STORY

Matt and I weren't sure where the tradition of bridesmaids and groomsmen came from. (I'd heard of a medieval superstition that evil spirits would find the bride unless she was surrounded by equally dressed-up women.) While the idea of having an inner circle of close friends and family nearby sounded fun, we wanted the whole community to come together to help. So why did we opt for five friends and family members on each side? In part, we were excited by the prospect of honoring our closest friends and family with the distinction of being in the wedding party. We also thought we would be more relaxed during the ceremony if our closest friends surrounded us. Plus, we probably subconsciously thought our wedding might be too different if we didn't follow the wedding party pattern.

Beyond the wedding party, we asked dozens of friends and family members to help make our wedding happen. As we solidified our budget and tried to figure out the catering situation, it became strikingly clear that we would need to tap into the talents and energy of our friends and family to pull off a budget wedding. Vendors are expensive. Wedding vendors are often more expensive.

But it wasn't just about saving money. It was also about building community and connection and having fun. At one point in the planning process, The Knot sent me an e-mail that read, "The more involved your guests are in your wedding, the more they will enjoy themselves."

I couldn't have agreed more! In my experience, people are more invested and engaged in something when they help make it possible. We wanted our guests—our nearest and dearest friends and family—to be part of the wedding creation process. We started a new tab in our trusty Excel wedding planning spreadsheet: "Jobs." (I ignored the fact that The Knot's idea for involving your guests was to give them a detailed ceremony program.)

Here's the comprehensive list of wedding tasks we delegated. (The list started much more modestly and grew longer throughout the wedding planning process.)

- Photographers
- Officiant
- Sound manager
- Fajita chef
- Salsa chef
- Bean and corn salad chef
- Seven-layer dip chef
- Sous chefs (6)
- Hair stylist
- Paymaster (to collect money for lodging from guests)
- Traffic directors (2)

- Ushers (2)
- Alcohol manager
- Grocery delivery person
- Laundry manager (to wash cloth napkins between the welcome picnic and the reception)
- S'mores director
- Drink manager (for the welcome picnic)
- Drink manager (for the ceremony)
- Group photo director
- Ceremony program managers (3)
- Cake deliverer
- Florist
- Videographers (2)
- Light manager
- Seamstress

As a side benefit, it would be much more fun to work with friends than strangers. But we didn't want people to feel so overwhelmed with responsibility that they couldn't enjoy themselves. We wanted them to have a good time. We figured that if different people each took one small piece of the work, all those pieces would add up to an amazing wedding.

So instead of asking one friend to be in charge of photography, we asked three. That way, no single person had to bear the burden of capturing everything. To make sure our fajita maker could be part of the action while he was cooking, we put four grills right by the outdoor dining area. We asked another friend to be his sous chef and keep him company. During the reception, multiple people ended up around the grills, helping out as needed.

We were conscious of asking people in a way that gave them permission to say no. We told them that our first and foremost goal was their enjoyment. A few people did turn down our requests. But those who said yes truly seemed to feel connected to the wedding. In the end, we pulled off a wedding "for the people, by the people," with many more than we had initially asked coming forward to make it happen. Those moments are a huge part of our wedding day memories.

We also tried to create community with our wedding website. First and foremost, it served as a catchall for everything related to our wedding. We wanted guests to look there for information first. But we also wanted them to feel more connected to us and to each other through our website.

We already owned the domain name www.ofafeather.us, which cost a mere $7 per year. We searched and searched for a company that would give us a free wedding website (a lot of companies will) *and* let us use our own name. No luck. (I've since learned that you can redirect visitors from your own domain to your wedding website and use something called masking to hide the wedding website URL.)

We decided to create a free blog instead. We used wordpress.org, which allowed us to create multiple pages. The website included:

- The agenda for the weekend
- Information on accommodations
- Directions to the location
- Carpooling information (we encouraged guests to leave comments for each other about their arrival and departure times, as well as their e-mail addresses for contacting each other)
- Suggested attire ("Outdoor summer wedding attire [summer days in Colorado are in the 80s]; khakis, collared shirts or button-downs, sun dresses, skirts, dressy Capri pants, etc. [Read: Comfortable!] Don't forget your sunglasses. . . and your umbrella! Evenings can be chilly in the mountains of Colorado. Bring your bathing suit if you want to go in the hot tub!")
- Weather information
- A link to our registry
- An RSVP form
- Information on ourselves (who we are and what we do professionally and personally)
- Information on our dog
- A guestbook, which allowed guests to upload pictures of themselves and to write a couple lines of text to introduce themselves
- A photograph request (we wanted guests to upload their photos of the wedding to a shared Flickr account after the wedding)
- A poll (we asked guests to vote on their favorite frozen margarita flavor)
- Contact information, including our phone numbers and address, as well as contact information for the ceremony, reception, and accommodation sites

Additionally, we decided to make a wedding quilt from the fabric of family and friends, so we asked each person to mail us a small piece of fabric. We included the parameters, as well as our address.

Our website functioned as a hub of all things related to our wedding. Guests used the carpool coordination area, and more than one-quarter of them uploaded photos of themselves with brief introductions. Several guests visited the website often to look for updates. (I wish we had added an application that allowed guests to request their favorite songs to be played at the reception. That would have been another way to build community and connection through guest involvement.)

In the months leading up to the wedding, we sent out e-mail updates reminding guests to RSVP, upload their profiles, and send us fabric. We always included links to the wedding website for easy access. Looking at it from the perspective of a wedding guest, I always appreciate when people send out reminders about the URLs for their wedding websites. I usually misplace (or recycle!) the actual wedding invitation, so it's helpful to be reminded of how I can access the website. Once the website was up and running, we were ready to send out save-the-date messages, which we ended up doing via e-mail. Because so many of our friends and family are e-mail regulars (and those who aren't talk daily or weekly with those who are), we decided that e-mail and the Internet in general would be our primary forms of communication. Hooray for budget-friendly *and* eco-friendly options!

We spent a lot of time wording it just right. Here's what our save-the-date message said:

Matt and I are officially tying the knot.
We would be elated if you would join us!

The wedding festivities will be held:
Friday, July 18 to Sunday, July 20, 2008

Outside of Estes Park, CO
(about 1.5 hours from the Denver International Airport)

Accommodations will likely cost:
Between $35–$80 per person per night

Action Requested:
Please respond to a brief survey by clicking on the link below.

We also decided to create an online survey to get a preliminary sense of who was coming and where they wanted to stay. Here's what the survey said:

Please enter your name:

What is the likelihood that you will be able to attend the shindig?

- ☐ *Barring any natural disasters or airline strikes, I'll be there! It is decidedly so.*
- ☐ *I'm about 75% sure I'll be there. Outlook good.*
- ☐ *I'm 50/50. I'll have to check the calendar. Ask again later.*
- ☐ *Sorry, I love ya, but the outlook is not so good.*

Comments/Questions/Addendums:

Will you be bringing a guest?

Where would you prefer to stay?

- ☐ *At the reception site in rustic cabins with up to 6 people in shared rooms for $35/person/night (includes breakfast); http://sunshinemtinn.com (this is where Matt and Sara will be staying)*
- ☐ *At the ceremony site approximately 6 miles away for $60–$246 per room or cabin, per night (includes breakfast); http://www.meekerparklodge.com*
- ☐ *At a free campsite nearby*

OPTIONAL: If you have any special skills or resources you would like to contribute to the wedding, please enter them below (think hard and be creative!)

OPTIONAL: What should Matt wear during the ceremony?

- ☐ *A wet suit*
- ☐ *His rainbow thong*
- ☐ *A kilt*
- ☐ *Anything spandex*
- ☐ *Other (please enter the attire of your choice here)*

The survey helped us get a sense of how many people would be able to make it. Getting a rough number early on helped us figure out our venue and catering needs.

When it came time to set up another wedding staple—the registry—we were less certain about what to do. Don't get me wrong, I love presents! And I understand and appreciate the cultural practice of giving wedding gifts. But we didn't want our out-of-town guests to fork over hundreds of dollars for flights, accommodations, and transportation and then feel obligated to spend money on gifts. On the other hand, we knew that some guests would insist on giving us gifts, so we decided to set up a registry.

What we needed more than anything was money. We were gearing up to buy a house soon after the wedding and needed to amass large amounts of dough for our closing. We decided to go with , which gave us the option to register for cash to go toward our down payment. (This option was less than ideal because the website skims a percentage of the cash off the top.) The website also allowed us to register for items from specific stores' websites. We added things like an REI dog pack, gardening books, and sewing shears. Because we had already been living together, we had the household items we needed.

Here's how we worded the text of our registry:

> *Your presence (pun intended) at our wedding is gift enough. Seriously. We utterly and completely appreciate your willingness to make the trek. If you stubbornly insist that a gift is necessary, you are welcome to view our registry by clicking on the link below. But honestly, your presence is more than enough. We're not kidding!*

With save-the-date notices sent and registry details figured out, we were ready to work on the invitations. Matt and I wanted to be kind to the earth and our wallets, so we opted for postcards.

Not only are postcards less expensive (costing at least 24¢ less per stamp), they also produce less waste. We increased the eco-friendliness of our invitations by asking guests to RSVP from the wedding website. We also included our address, in case the less technologically savvy crowd wanted alternate means for RSVP-ing.

We went further with the eco- and budget-friendliness by using paper we already had on hand. We used watercolor paper, cut into 4x6 cards.

Matt and I took turns suggesting designs for the invitations. I would draw something and show it to him, and he would incorporate my design into his drawing. Then he would show his drawing to me, and I would incorporate his design into my next version. Since our Web address was http://ofafeather.us, a bird theme began to emerge unintentionally. Eventually, we agreed on a tree and two birds on the front of the invitation, with the following text:

Birds of a Feather, please flock together
to celebrate the marriage of Matt Bradford and Sara Cotner . . .

Saturday, July 19, 2008; 4:00pm
Allenspark, Colorado

For more information and to RSVP (by 6/1/08) in an environmentally friendly way, please visit http://ofafeather.us or send a note to 2428 Benton Street; Edgewater, CO 80214.

On the back of the card, we opted for a leaf design, the recipient's address, and personal messages from both of us. Although we had never seen a wedding invitation with personal messages to the recipients, this piece was important to us. We wanted our guests to feel valued, loved, and appreciated.

Producing the invitations took quite a bit of time (as do most DIY projects), but the process helped us slow down, focus on the event and what it meant to us, and think about each and every guest.

I desperately wanted to complete the personalized look with photo stamps. I thought a picture of us would be utterly perfect. However, we had budgeted only $50 for invitations, and photo stamps would have put us over budget. Oh, how I wanted those stamps! The only alternative was regular postcard stamps from the U.S. Postal Service. At the time, USPS was offering only Florida panther stamps.

Matt helped talk me down from the ledge of irrationality. Cue my wedding mantras! Whenever I started to feel slightly crazed and started to blur the distinction between needs and wants, I asked myself: "When my wedding is said and done and I've settled into marriage, will I still care about _________?"

In the end, the invitations weren't stunningly beautiful. But they were the most heartfelt and sincere invitations we could produce, and people told us they especially appreciated the personalized messages.

Plus, we came in under budget. The extra money was a welcome relief, because every other line of the budget felt insanely tight.

THE WEDDING PARTY

The wedding party is another aspect of a wedding where you can forge your own path, no matter how ingrained the traditions feel. Possible options include:

- No wedding party. Ceremonies can be more intimate and sincere with just the bride, groom, and officiant. If you want other people involved,

they can come up at various times to do readings, sing songs, light candles, or hand over the rings.

- A wedding party of family. Instead of surrounding yourself with friends, opt to surround yourself with family members. The benefit is that your relationship with the wedding party will withstand the tests of time and distance (probably).
- A small wedding party. Instead of a line of friends and family members trailing behind you, you might decide to select one friend or family member to keep you company.
- A large wedding party. If you'll feel more comfortable surrounding yourself with lots of friends and family members, go for it. (And you don't need an equal number of people on each side.)
- The entire audience as your wedding party. You can stand everyone in a circle so that all guests feel as if they're part of the ceremony.

Selecting the wedding party can easily become an area of contention. Your family might think it would be rude not to ask your cousin to participate. A toxic friend might expect a spot simply because she asked you to be in her wedding. It can definitely be tricky figuring out how to balance others' wants with your wants and needs.

My general philosophy is: It's your wedding. Everyone should get to plan her own wedding. Period. You plan your wedding and let your friends, children, colleagues, and neighbors plan their own weddings, okay?

With that said, I understand that the ideal might not match up with the reality. Maybe you'd rather concede to someone else's ideas about your wedding party than get into an argument about it. That's okay too. The important thing is to avoid regret as much as possible. If including your cousin in the wedding party is going to make you feel uncomfortable, don't do it. However, if you apply the 10-10-10 Rule and think your relationship with someone not included in the wedding party will still be negatively affected ten years later, maybe it's worth the compromise.

Think about whom you want in your wedding party and why. If others have a different perspective, dig into their reasons, then make a decision that feels right to you and your partner. And after that? Be done with it. The wedding planning to-do list is long, and you'll drive yourself crazy if you second-guess every decision.

DELEGATING, DELEGATING, DELEGATING

Tapping into the talents of friends and family can save you some serious money. Photographers, deejays, hair stylists, caterers, and other wedding vendors charge thousands of dollars. Even replacing one traditional wedding vendor with a family member or friend could save you a mortgage payment (or two).

But more than that, asking friends and family to help with your wedding planning and execution can transform your wedding experience from a stressful endeavor for you and a passive show for your guests into a meaningful and memorable celebration of love, commitment, and fun for everyone. When you ask your nearest and dearest to help, you give them an opportunity to share their talents and show their love for you. When you make a wedding a group effort, you build community and connection. When you surround yourself with people you love instead of people you've hired, you get to the very center of what marriage is and what a wedding has the potential to be.

Elizabeth, a nanny from Indiana, knows firsthand about the benefits of asking for help. Her mother helped from day one of the engagement, while a friend lent sound equipment and "even stepped up to act as a deejay." Another friend played guitar during the ceremony, and her father-in-law "even made his well-known and loved chicken for the reception." She explained that it "helped save money, yes." But mostly, she loves "the concept of a wedding community." For her, "the day was so filled with love and significance because so many people brought their unique talents and resources to the table to celebrate the start of marriage."

GETTING OVER THE GUILT OF ASKING PEOPLE TO HELP

During the American frontier days, settlers held bees to accomplish daunting tasks that they couldn't accomplish alone. They invited friends and neighbors over to help clear timber, raise barns, harvest crops, and shuck corn. Bees were an opportunity to get a lot of work done in a short amount of time, as well as an opportunity to socialize. I love this idea of people coming together to help each other. I think we should apply the same concept to weddings.

However, a lot of brides-to-be tell me they feel guilty asking their guests to help out at their weddings. The top concern is that guests will be too busy working to have any fun, and it's a reasonable one. However, there are ways to structure jobs to ensure that guests can still fully participate in all the fun. A simple strategy is to break each job into very small tasks or shifts, so that no single person is left bearing too much responsibility. For example, instead of asking someone to deejay the whole reception, ask five friends to take an hour each.

Sample List of Roles

Possible Jobs	Check if Needed	Possible Friends/Family Members to Ask
Photographer	☐	
Officiant	☐	
Sound manager	☐	
Emcee	☐	
Chef	☐	
Hair stylist	☐	
Traffic director	☐	
Ushers	☐	
Bartender	☐	
Group photo director	☐	
Ceremony program manager	☐	
Cake deliverer	☐	
Florist	☐	
Videographer	☐	
Light manager	☐	
Seamstress	☐	
Ceremony musicians	☐	

Ivy, a community organizer from Massachusetts, broke the responsibilities down into many small jobs that ranged from "Fun Captain (making sure people danced) to leading a hike to planning the menu and cooking the food." She also asked three people who knew the overall plan to be in charge of "fielding questions and problem solving." In the end, asking people to help encouraged her friends to get "to know each other very well," and "people were proud of what they contributed."

People also hesitate to ask friends and family to help because it somehow feels inappropriate or rude, as though you're using your guests like hired help. However, the reality is often just the opposite. Think of asking for help as saying, "We value, love, and appreciate you so much that we want you right by our sides as we create our wedding; we honestly couldn't do it without you."

When asking for help, make sure to:

- Make saying no an option. It's easy for friends and family to feel obligated to help when asked. To be respectful and to ensure the smoothest wedding experience possible, make people feel completely comfortable saying no if they don't want to help.
- Not treat people like hired help. Of course, you wouldn't treat anyone poorly, even if you were paying them, but keep in mind that your friends and family are volunteering their time and energy to help you. They don't deserve to be subjected to any tantrums, sighs, complaints, or any frustration related to their work.
- Accept their best as good enough. In other words, elevate the process above the product. If your friend volunteers to make boutonnieres but accidentally uses three pieces of fern instead of two, set aside your vision (and frustration). Remember that getting help from a friend who cares about you is more beautiful than a boutonniere with two pieces of fern will ever be. It takes an immense amount of self-discipline, maturity, and awareness to step out of the moment and focus on the big picture, but that's what this whole process is about.
- Show your appreciation—often and sincerely. As your friends and family devote time and energy to helping you, set aside a moment to stop giving directions and to give them a sincere thank you.

THE WEDDING WEBSITE

In our house, the shelf by the front door tends to serve as the catchall. It catches our keys, cell phones, wallets—the list goes on. If we're ever looking for something important, we look there first.

A wedding website should function as the same kind of catchall. It should include any and all information that guests could possibly need to get to and from your wedding, figure out what to bring, and understand how they are going to spend their time. Wedding websites also allow you to provide lots of information without spending extra money on invitation inserts and postage. Here are some questions that your website might answer for guests:

- What airport do I fly into?
- What time do I need to arrive?
- Where do I need to show up?
- Is there anything special I should know about parking?
- What should I wear?
- Will we be inside or outside?
- Will the reception be in the same place as the ceremony?
- How long will the party last?
- Should I expect to eat? What will my options be?
- Where are you registered?
- Which meals will be included?
- What is there to do in town when I'm not attending the wedding?

The site could also answer more personal questions, such as:

- How did you meet?
- How long have you been dating?
- What's your proposal story?
- What does your partner do for a living and for fun?
- Who is in your wedding party?

You have several options for creating a wedding website. First, you could start a blog. Many blogs are free and easy to create. You can capitalize on the blog function by updating your guest list along the way (with static pages that include all other information), or you can set up the blog to look like a static website. You can even purchase your own domain name, such as http://lillianandben.com, for about $10 from a company such as Name.com.

Another option is to use a template from a wedding site. The benefit of this route is that the templates are designed specifically for weddings, so you don't have to get too creative or think too hard about putting the material together.

To make the most of your wedding website, try not to stress about it. When you apply the 10-10-10 Rule to your website, you are likely to admit that the quality of the site might matter in ten minutes and maybe ten months (depending on when your wedding is) but definitely not in ten years. And the things that are likely to cause you stress (such as the aesthetics of the site) are the things that will matter least to your guests. Your guests care about the information. They want their questions answered quickly and easily.

Your most organized guests will receive the invitation in the mail and promptly record the wedding website URL in their planners. Less organized guests will find a magnet and stick the invitation on the fridge. A big chunk of guests might leave the invitation on the table (to get buried beneath the water bill and restaurant receipts). Do your guests (and yourself) a favor by periodically reminding them about your website URL. E-mail is probably the best way to communicate such information. For a few people, a phone call will suffice.

Wedding websites can also be used interactively, as a two-way communication channel between you and your guests. For example, you could set up an online RSVP. You could also set up a form that allows guests to submit their favorite songs to be included in the dance mix.

SAVE-THE-DATE NOTICES

Once you've nailed down your wedding date and location, put together a save-the-date notice to inform guests as early as possible. Victoria and her partner, Joe, "used a free e-mail marketing program called MailChimp—it has an HTML editor and can manage all your guest e-mail addresses, provide view/click stats, etc." But Gretchen and her partner, Andrew, opted not to use save-the-date notices at all because they sent out invitations well ahead of the wedding.

If you're not careful, save-the-date notices can lose their practicality and morph into a giant monster that feeds on your time, money, energy, and sanity. Ellie, a lawyer from Baltimore, decided to make save-the-date coasters. She explained, "My husband collects beer mats, so we got a stamp set and a custom stamp with our wedding date and website on it and made sets of two coasters. We hand delivered most of them, to save on postage, but that was a bad idea because we didn't keep track of who got one. Also, nobody used them as coasters; they all just stuck them on the fridge, so we probably should have just sent postcards."

Since save-the-date notices are one of the first things you invest time and energy in, you may be tempted to go all out. You might be itching to get creative or to make a good impression. Think critically about your approach here. Your wedding planning process is just starting. If you invest time, energy, and money in this project, what will you have left when you're on the fortieth item on your wedding to-do list? Will you be frazzled, frustrated, and disconnected from the real purpose of a wedding? To keep things simple, consider these options:

- Send e-mails
- Use a service that sends electronic save-the-date messages, such as Pingg.com
- Send save-the-date postcards in lieu of invitations (include the URL of your wedding website and explain that you will be updating the site as the wedding gets closer)

If you want to get a little fancier and spend more time, effort, and money, consider these save-the-date options:

- Vintage postcards from the town where your wedding will take place (you can print the information on labels and affix them to the cards, so you don't have to write all the information by hand)
- Themed objects, such as origami boats for a wedding by the lake or a piece of rope tied in a knot to announce that you're tying the knot
- 4x6 photographs (you can slap stamps on them and send them through the mail like postcards)
- A video uploaded to the Internet
- Stationery from a craft supply store
- A postcard made via an online printer, such as Vistaprint

INVITATIONS

When it comes to wedding invitations, you have many options. The choices vary remarkably in terms of cost, effort, and environmental impact. They include:

- Ready-made stationery. Stores such as Target, Michaels, and OfficeMax sell predesigned invitations that you can customize with your own text, then print at home. It's very economical and easy.
- Downloadable invitations. Online design companies such as e.m. papers are popping up all the time. You can pay a flat fee and download invitations, as well as save-the-date cards and RSVP cards. You can print the documents at home or upload them to an online printer.

- DIY invitations. Making your own invitations isn't as hard as it might seem. You can use stamps, a color printer, stickers, and other tools.
- Professionally designed invitations. Online clearinghouses for independent artisans—such as Etsy.com—showcase lots of independent designers who do good work for good prices.
- Outside-the-box invitations. You might consider sending vintage postcards, a poster in a tube, or a tin of Lemonhead candies.

In the end, remember that most of your guests don't care about the invitations nearly as much as you do. They just want to know the who, what, where, and when.

THE REGISTRY

The registry can be easy or hard, depending on your feelings, perspective, and life situation. You might feel uncomfortable asking guests for gifts, especially if they have to spend a lot of time and energy traveling to your wedding. You might not be sure what to register for, especially if you're already well stocked in the housewares department. You might wonder how to ask for things you really want, such as money for your honeymoon or for a down payment on a house. You might also consider suggesting that guests donate to charity in lieu of sending you gifts.

And while you and your partner have ideas swirling around in your heads, your guests might have different ideas. Perhaps you feel uncomfortable with gifts, but guests feel uncomfortable if they don't give a gift. A registry can help guests better understand your tastes and preferences and choose something you will truly appreciate and use. For out-of-town guests who have to spend significant money to attend your wedding, an optional registry is perfect. You're not expecting gifts, but if your guests want to give you something, they know where to start.

When it comes to creating a registry, there are many routes to take:

- The in-store route. Many stores will provide you with a scanner for choosing which items you want added to your registry. When guests go to the store, they receive a printout of your registry. Feel free to include anything that you need and want—not just housewares. Be sure to provide options at all different price levels.
- Registering online. If most of your guest list is tech savvy, you might opt for a registry that lets you include links from all over the Web in a centralized place. For example, Amazon.com lets you add anything from any online store into your registry.

- A charity or hybrid gift/charity registry. You can register for gifts and do good for others at the same time. The I Do Foundation (www.idofoundation.org) and other groups often partner with businesses such as Target and REI. When someone purchases a gift through your registry, up to 10 percent of the purchase price goes to the charities of your choice. An alternative gift registry (www.alternativegiftregistry.org) combines traditional gifts, donations to charity, and special gifts such as family recipes and homemade pies for the wedding reception.
- Funding your honeymoon. Sites such as www.honeyfund.com allow guests to pay for different aspects of your honeymoon, such as plane fare, cocktails, or surfing lessons.

Of course, you can combine various options to create a registry hybrid that works for you. (Or you can opt out of the registry idea altogether.) Come up with a plan that strikes a balance between your comfort and your guests' comfort.

WEDDING SHOWERS

Wedding showers, like registries, are a way for people to give gifts to you and your partner. However, being in-person events, showers make you the center of attention in a very immediate way. You might feel uncomfortable having a party thrown in your honor, but your friends and family might want another opportunity to celebrate you and to show their love and support. If there is a discrepancy between what you want and what family and friends want to do for you, set aside some time for introspection.

If you're feeling overwhelmed and stressed by the wedding planning process, it can be a relief to forgo wedding showers altogether. Alternatively, if you're uncomfortable with the traditional format and gift focus of showers but you're still eager to get together with friends and family, consider doing something entirely different, such as bowling or a DIY party to accomplish wedding projects. As with all things wedding-related, you have to separate out what others expect versus the most authentic, joyful path for you.

IDEAS FOR NEXT STEPS

- Decide what kind of wedding party works for you. Do you want to be alone with your partner? Do you want to be surrounded by your parents and other family members rather than friends? Do you want your pets in the wedding party? There are no rules. Do what makes sense for you.

- Brainstorm ways that your family and friends can help with the wedding itself. Collaborating and sharing the load will save money, help build community and connection, and help create a meaningful and memorable wedding. Make a specific list of tasks and possible helpers, taking into account the talents and interests you already know about. Then start asking.
- Set up a wedding website to serve as a hub of information about your wedding. It can be as elaborate or as simple as you want. As you create the site, ask yourself: "If I were a guest, what would I want and need to know?" The more information you can provide, and the sooner you get the website up, the easier you'll make it for your guests, especially those who will travel to your wedding. You may want to prioritize function over form to get the website up faster.
- Create and send save-the-date notices. The sooner you can send them the better.
- Find (or create from scratch) wedding invitation language that reflects you as a couple. Just as there's no set formula for your actual wedding, your invitations can be whatever you want them to be.
- Make a decision about the registry. You have plenty of options, so figure out what makes the most sense for you as a couple (and for your friends and family).
- Decide whether or not you're comfortable with a wedding shower (consult your partner) and politely communicate your decision to the appropriate people.
- Consult your wedding vision to align your choices with what you and your partner want. Use your wedding mantras to stay on track.
- Have fun and conserve your energy. There's still a lot left to do!

DIY Project 2:

A PERSONALIZED STAMP

A personalized stamp can come in handy for a host of projects. Use it to embellish your invitation envelopes, brand wedding favors, or add a personal touch to table numbers. Making your own stamp is easier than you might think, and the price is right.

MATERIALS

A block of soft, white eraser-like material—such as Blick E-Z-Cut Printing Blocks—from an art supply store (large enough for your design)

A package of stamp-carving tools

An ink pad and ink in whatever color you like. (If you want to use the stamp for more than one color, buy multiple inks, multiple ink pads, and a solvent to clean the stamp.)

A regular #2 pencil (not a mechanical pencil)

DIRECTIONS

1. Choose the image you want to create with your stamp. The less intricate the design and the thicker the lines, the easier it will be to carve. You can design your image on the computer and transfer it to your stamp or draw it directly on the rubber.
2. If you want to transfer a printed image to your stamp, trace the lines of the design with a pencil to get lead on the lines.
3. Place the image face-down on the rubber and tape it in place if necessary.
4. Use the pencil to rub over the back of your image (as though you are coloring the back of the image). The pressure will transfer the image from the front of the paper onto the rubber.
5. Use stamp-carving tools to carve away the rubber around the lines of your design. Use small tools to cut around the lines and big tools to carve out large chunks of background space.
6. When you think you've carved out enough rubber, test your stamp by pushing it onto an ink pad and pressing it onto paper. If you haven't carved enough rubber, you will see unwanted spots in your image. Use your tools to carve away those areas.

Tip: Remember that stamps are mirror images, so you need to carve your design in reverse. If you transfer your design from paper using the process described above, the design will automatically show up in reverse. If you are drawing directly on the rubber, your images and words need to be reversed. For example, you would write "love" as "svol." To check your image before carving your stamp, hold it in front of a mirror.

Mercury ELECTRIC
celebrate
LAURA + JOE
are tying the knot
and would be ecstatic to see you
AUGUST 9, 2014
3:00 p.m. ▪ LIVE OAKS FRIENDS MEETING HOUSE
1318 West 26th Street ▪ Houston, Texas 77008 ▪
RSVP and more information @ http://lauraplusjoe.com

DIY Project 3:
INVITATIONS

DIY invitations can be a very satisfying project. Setting aside time to individually craft each card and send it to a dear friend or family member can help you slow down and focus on the present moment. This project is particularly appealing because it's inexpensive and relatively easy to implement. It's even more fun if friends and family help you.

Tips

- Consider writing your guests personal notes, so they know you're thinking about them and hoping they can make it.
- Instead of circles, try a different shape. (More cutters are available in the scrapbooking section of craft stores.)
- Print addresses directly on envelopes in a handwritten font. One of my favorite free fonts is Scriptina.
- Read the directions that come with your circle cutter to produce the best possible circles.
- Play with different stitches to create various effects.

MATERIALS

Paint chips (sample colors from a home improvement store)
Printer (home or professional)
Cardstock (90- to 110-pound stock, depending on what your printer can handle)
Paper cutter, scissors, or a craft knife
Circle cutter or circle punch (approximately 1 inch in diameter)
Glue stick
Sewing machine
Thread
Envelopes (A7; 5¼x7¼ inch)
Optional: corner rounder

DIRECTIONS

1. Use any word processing program or something fancier, such as InDesign, to design the text. You can download a template at http://2000dollarwedding.com/p/project-templates.html.

   Use black-and-white text to cut down on cost.
2. Lay out two 5x7 invitations on each page, with a horizontal orientation.
3. Print your invitations on cardstock, either on a home printer or by uploading them to a professional printing service, such as FedEx Office or Vistaprint.
4. Cut out the invitations using a craft knife, paper cutter, or scissors.
5. Using a circle cutter or a circle punch, cut out paint chips approximately 1 inch in diameter.
6. Use a small bit of glue to secure each circle in place (before you run it through the sewing machine).
7. Sew a straight line through the circles to secure them.
8. For a more finished and professional look, clip the corners with a corner rounder.

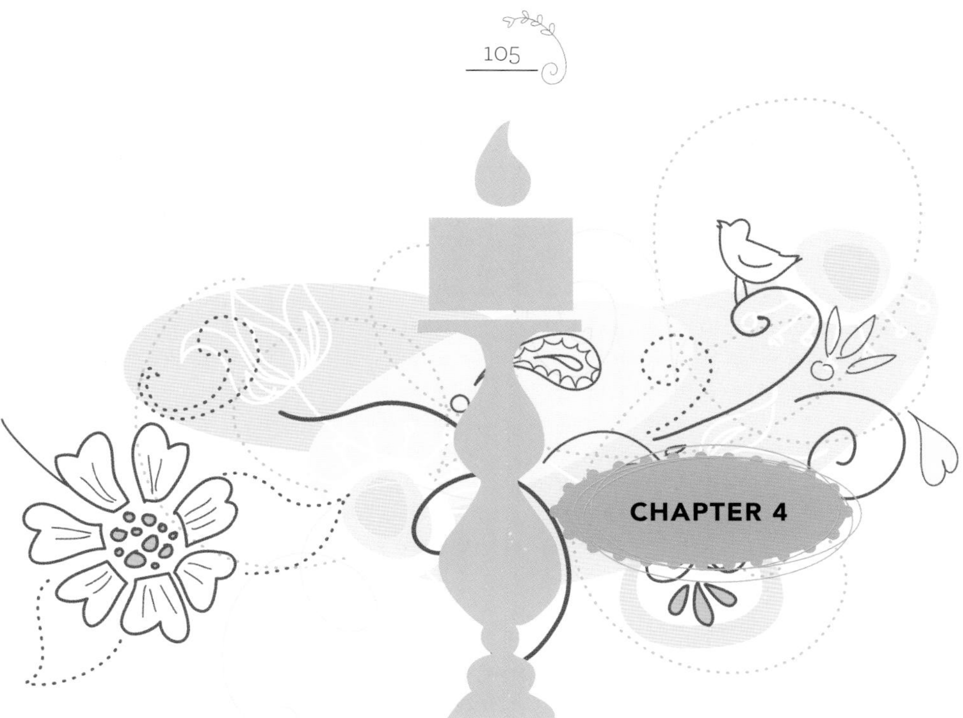

THE HEART OF THE MATTER: Planning the Ceremony

When some of the major pieces of your wedding are in place, it's time to shift focus to the heart of your wedding: the ceremony. Once again, we start with the end vision (including a ceremony vision worksheet). In this chapter, we cover how to write your own ceremony and create your own traditions and rituals, if you want to go that route. We also include strategies for avoiding the spotlight if you're hesitant to be the center of attention. We address the details of ceremony flowers, music, programs, and ring pillows. DIY projects include ceremony program fans, a wedding quilt duvet cover, a ring pillow, and boutonnieres.

OUR STORY

I'm embarrassed to admit that Matt and I procrastinated when it came to writing our ceremony. I believe that the ceremony is one of the most important aspects of the wedding and wedding planning. But writing the ceremony takes some emotional and creative effort, and it's easier to spend time browsing the Internet for dresses and rings.

Creating a meaningful and memorable ceremony is challenging—really challenging. Matt and I decided that we would brainstorm ideas together. Then I would draft something and we would revise it together.

When we sat down to brainstorm, we started with the end in mind. We wanted our ceremony to focus on community, commitment, connection, and fun. We freed ourselves from standard ceremony templates and thought about things that represented these four goals. We wanted to split up the speaking among Matt, me, and Andy, our friend and officiant, so that one person's voice didn't dominate the entire ceremony.

For the introduction, we wanted to focus on our families and friends. I found a quote about friendship through a Google search and wrote the introduction around that quote. Andy gave the introduction:

> *Welcome and thank you for joining us as we celebrate Matt and Sara's commitment to one another. As French writer Marcel Proust said, "Let us be grateful to people who make us happy; they are the charming gardeners who make our souls blossom." You are the people who make the souls of Sara and Matt blossom. We want to acknowledge and thank all of you for your support and participation today.*

We wanted to acknowledge and thank family members and friends personally, but we didn't want the ceremony to last longer than thirty minutes. We thought about writing everyone a note to let them know how much they meant to us and asking them to open it and read it during the ceremony. We decided against the idea because we had already written them personal notes on the invitations (and we would also be writing personal notes on thank-you cards). So we balanced personalization with the need for efficiency by having Andy say:

> *We have family members from both sides: Indiana, Michigan, Florida, Connecticut, and California. We have Matt's friends: college, camp, KIPP, childhood, and Denver. Sara's friends: college, Teach for America, KIPP, and Denison Montessori.*

While I was searching for quotes on friendship, I came across another one I really liked. Matt and I couldn't decide between the Proust one and this one, so we included them both. Andy continued:

> *These friends, a famous writer once wrote, represent "a world in us, a world possibly not born until they arrive, and it is only by this meeting that a new world is born." Each of you has been invited to participate in this commitment ceremony because you have, in some way, brought about a new world in Sara or Matt.*

While I was researching other people's ceremonies online, I came across the idea of giving a flower to the mom on each side. We decided, instead, to give out hugs and walked into the audience to hug first our own families, then each other's family members. Here's what we said:

> ***Sara.***
> *We would especially like to thank our families who have nurtured our independence . . .*
>
> ***Matt.***
> *. . . and have put up with our quirkiness.*
>
> *[Sara and Matt walk into the audience to hug their own families.]*
>
> ***Matt.***
> *And we would also like to thank each other's family for welcoming us so kindly . . .*
>
> ***Sara.***
> *. . . and for putting up with our quirkiness.*
>
> *[Sara and Matt walk into the audience to hug the other's family.]*

We wanted to say something that acknowledged the injustice of same-sex marriage bans. At first, Matt was hesitant about including this piece (even though he wholeheartedly supports same-sex marriage) because he didn't want to upset some of his Irish Catholic family members. Andy intervened by suggesting that we rephrase our comments to make them positive rather than negative. Here's what we ended up with:

Matt.
As we gather here to solidify our commitment to each other, we would also like to celebrate the fact that California just joined the ranks of Massachusetts by finally starting to extend the rights and privileges of marriage to everyone, regardless of sexual orientation.

Sara.
It moves us one step closer to fulfilling our nation's promise to provide liberty and justice for all.

The next part of the ceremony was a cross between a Quaker meeting and a reception toasting. At a Quaker meeting, guests speak when they feel moved to say something. We loved the idea of different people saying different things, but we wanted the speeches to be somewhat prepared, and we wanted a little control over the situation (for example, we wanted the speakers to be balanced between my friends and family and his). We didn't want to be the center of attention all night long, so we didn't want traditional toasts. However, since we like toasts, we decided to move them into the ceremony.

We decided to have five friends and family members prepare two-minute speeches. We left the content fairly open, suggesting they read poems, make a toast, or share a memory. Each person's speech was personal, sincere, and authentic. Matt and I held each other while we listened to each speaker.

Then we had a tree-planting ceremony. We planted a sapling in a pot. We would later transplant the tree to the backyard at our first house. I did some research to figure out what different trees symbolize and what type of tree to get. The result:

Andy.
Now Matt and Sara are going to plant a live oak sapling from the backyard of Sara's family to symbolically represent the growth of their love.

In early America, live oaks were widely used to build planks in ships because of their remarkable resilience. The live oak of the USS Constitution *repelled the shot of enemy gunfire so effectively that one of the sailors was heard to shout, "Huzzah! Her sides are made of iron!" The ship was given the nickname Old Ironsides.*

Like the planks on ships, marriage, too, must be resilient. It must weather the challenges of daily life and the passage of time. And just like the tree that they are planting, marriage requires constant

nurturing and nourishment. As they provide the sun, soil, and water for this tree, they will provide the encouragement, trust, and love needed on a daily basis to consciously nurture their connection to each other.

We wanted our vows to be sincere and fun. Here's what we said:

Sara.
Matt, I love you because you make me laugh out loud on a daily basis, like when you come up with alternate names for our dog, Hoss, such as Hoss-tage, Hoss of Pain, or Hoss-car Mayer Weiner.

I love you because you challenge me to be a better person, like when you made me promise to tell the Penske truck people that we scraped the moving van.

I love you because we create adventures together, like Halloween scavenger hunts or road trips out west.

I love you because you care so much for other people that you inspire all of us to be more caring. You do things like put toothpaste on my toothbrush and leave it out for me or come home on the worst day of winter with slippers and a Chia pet herb garden.

I love you because I smile every time I wake up to you and when I come home to you. We play together, brainstorm together, create together, read together. Your hand always feels comfortable in mine.

Matt, because I love you, I promise to treat you the way you want to be treated and with the respect you deserve. I promise to build trust with my words and actions. I will be your cheerleader, your nurse, your editor, your therapist, your teacher, your student, and your partner in adventure. I will deeply appreciate all of your positive qualities and not let the passage of time dull that appreciation. When life challenges us, I promise to focus on the resiliency of our love. And if I stumble and fail to live up to my promises, I will look you in the eyes, hold your hands, and apologize with sincerity. I will be my best for you.

Matt.
Sara, I love you because you are always working to make yourself and the world better; sending birthday cards to friends and reading self-help books.

I love you because you never settle for one opinion; you ask friends, family, and consult articles and books.

I love you because you stand up for what you believe in; like when you spoke up to your assistant principal about what was working, what was not, and the ways that you could work to change it.

I love you because you create documents, documents, documents to better your life and the lives of others; like when we copied over ninety thousand documents from your old computer.

I love you because you make up songs about our dog, your butt, and my smells, and they sound good.

Sara, because I love you, I promise to treat you the way you want to be treated and with the respect you deserve. I promise to build trust with my words and actions. I will be your cheerleader, your nurse, your editor, your therapist, your teacher, your student, and your partner in adventure. I will deeply appreciate all of your positive qualities and not let the passage of time dull that appreciation. When life challenges us, I promise to focus on the resiliency of our love. And if I stumble and fail to live up to my promises, I will look you in the eyes, hold your hands, and apologize with sincerity. I will be my best for you.

Andy.

In Swahili, the word ubuntu *means "My humanity is bound up with yours." From their vows to each other, it is very clear that Sara and Matt's humanities are bound up with each other. But they both recognize that their humanity is also bound up with that of the world. As the author of* The Little Prince *says, "Life has taught us that love does not consist in gazing at each other, but in looking outward together in the same direction."*

Now they will make vows to the world.

Matt.

We will develop in ourselves and inspire in others environmental consciousness . . .

Sara.

. . . honest and nurturing interpersonal connections . . .

Matt.

. . . and an active commitment to make the world more just for all.

Then it was time to exchange rings. I did some more research about the symbolism of rings and incorporated it into the ceremony:

Andy.

Now Matt and Sara will exchange rings to embody the commitments they have made to each other and the world.

Just as circles contain no end and no beginning, these rings are linked to the past and the future. They are connected to the headpiece that Matt's grandmother wore during her wedding fifty-four years ago, and they are made from the recycled metal of old jewelry from friends and family. They are worn on the third finger because of an ancient Greek belief that a vein from that finger goes directly to the heart.

Matt.
[Sara puts Matt's ring on his finger.] I will wear this ring as a celebration of our commitments to each other and the world.

Sara.
[Matt puts Sara's ring on her finger.] I will wear this ring as a celebration of our commitments to each other and the world.

Finally, we decided to symbolize unity through a quilt wrapping. During my research, I had read about Jewish chuppahs quilted from the fabric of friends and family. I had also read about a wedding where the couple was wrapped in a blanket. We put the two ideas together in this way:

Andy.
In the Jewish tradition, marriages take place under a chuppah, which can be constructed from the fabric of friends and family. In some Native American traditions, couples are wrapped in a blanket to signify their coming together and their new life together. [Brent and Mike take the quilt out of the basket and hold it up for everyone to see.]

In this symbolic gesture signifying unification, Matt and Sara will be wrapped in a quilt made from fabric from all of you, their family and friends. [Brent and Mike wrap Sara and Matt in the quilt.]

This quilt signifies the warmth and support of family and friends that are needed to sustain a healthy relationship. It signifies the bond between Matt and Sara and the closeness that will continue to develop day after day. It signifies the comfort and beauty they bring to each other and will continue to bring to each other. Together within this blanket, they will sign their marriage into being. [Sara and Matt sign the contract. Mike and Brent remove the quilt.]

Now they will embrace and kiss to celebrate that they are now officially united.

While we were figuring out the ceremony, we brainstormed ways to deflect being the center of attention. Here's what we did:

- We didn't walk down the aisle. First of all, there wasn't an aisle to walk down. I worried about it for a few seconds. Then I realized, "Wait a second. I don't actually want to walk down an aisle. I'll already be nervous about speaking in front of everybody; I would rather forgo the expected aisle altogether." We simply pulled up in our car, got out, and started mingling with our guests. I was nervous for about two seconds. Then I saw my good friend Luis and got overwhelmed with love and affection for him. I pretty much stopped feeling nervous. People were naturally looking at me and my dress, but I was too busy talking with people to notice much.
- We eliminated toasts during the reception. We love toasts, but we didn't want to stop in the middle of the party and focus attention back on us.
- We decided to use the cake cutting as an opportunity to thank our friends and family for helping with the wedding rather than for drawing more attention to ourselves.
- We planned simultaneous activities to take place during the reception so that people could do their own thing instead of waiting to see what we were doing. We had dancing on the patio, board games in the living room, a hot tub, and marshmallows roasting around a campfire. We posted a sign with all the activities, so people knew what options were available.
- We limited the guest list to our nearest and dearest rather than a large circle of acquaintances.

In the end, it was the perfect ceremony *for us*. It wasn't the ceremony my grandparents would have wanted for us. Nor was it a ceremony that people had seen before, but it was exactly what we wanted. People seemed to enjoy it because they love us, and because it so closely represented who we are and what we value. The more authentic your ceremony is, the more connected you are likely to feel to your own wedding.

ESTABLISHING A CEREMONY VISION

The ceremony is at the core of the wedding and the core of the marriage. However, it's not given much attention in mainstream wedding planning. Because it's not monetized and can be emotionally loaded, it's easy to neglect the ceremony or give it short shrift. I put the ceremony earlier in this book than you will find it in other planning guides to emphasize its gravity. The

earlier you focus on the ceremony, the more you and your partner can devote thoughtful attention to it.

Just as you created a wedding vision, consider creating a ceremony vision to guide your choices. Working with your partner, think about questions like: What does the ceremony mean to us? What do we want to think, feel, and do during the ceremony? What have we seen and heard at other weddings that struck a chord inside us? What do we want our guests to think, feel, and do as a result of witnessing our ceremony?

Since a ceremony is mostly words, you might find working with favorite quotes helpful. What speaks to you about a certain quote? You and your partner might also try free-writing. In free-writing, you write without stopping. If you get stuck, you can either repeat a word over and over or write something like, "I have no idea what else to say." Both you and your partner should do ten minutes of separate free-writing. Then come back together and discuss what you've written. You might uncover ideas or perspectives you didn't even know existed.

WRITING YOUR OWN CEREMONY

If you want to write your own ceremony, great. If you don't, that's great too. Make the choice that works for you and your partner and aligns with the ceremony vision you've created.

Find or write words that make sense to you and your partner. It doesn't matter if you use a standard script provided by your church, something you read on the Internet, or your own writing. Your ceremony is *your* ceremony. (Just don't charge admission or you might get sued for copyright infringement.)

If you decide to write your own ceremony, here are some pointers:

- Go back to your vision. It's easy to get stuck while writing and forget to look back at your ceremony vision for inspiration. Your vision should give you ideas about what you want to say and do during your ceremony.
- Think outside the box (if you want to). There are no rules about what a ceremony has to be. If you want to play paper-rock-scissors in the middle of your ceremony to decide who speaks first, go for it.
- Dig deep for inspiration. What writings resonate with you? Texts from college? Old sayings? Poems? Children's books? Fortunes from a cookie? Anything and everything can be fodder or inspiration for your ceremony.
- Scour the Internet. You can stand on the shoulders of those who have gone before you. You'll find many scripts to browse through online. Feel free to make liberal use of your computer's copy and paste functions. As long as it has meaning to you, it doesn't matter who wrote it.

Ceremony Vision Worksheet

What would you like to say about your ceremony after it's over?

What would your partner like to say about your wedding after it's over?

What would you want to overhear someone say about your ceremony?

Which adjectives would you like to describe your ceremony?

Your List	Your Partner's List

Which elements from other ceremonies would you like to incorporate?

Which elements from other ceremonies would you like to avoid?

- Just get a draft down on paper. Writing is a process. Your final version might bear no resemblance to your first pass. That fact can be extremely liberating. Just do your best to get something on paper and then worry about adding, deleting, replacing, or rearranging.

Remember that the ceremony is ultimately just words spoken aloud in front of people who love you and wish you happiness. Yes, the experience will be profound, but your marriage is bigger and deeper than those words. The words are only verbal vows and promises; it's through your actions every day that you will fulfill your intentions and live according to those words.

CREATING TRADITIONS AND RITUALS

My family is big into rituals and traditions. On Christmas Eve we always eat fondue and French fries. We also set the table with English "crackers" (twisted paper tubes with surprises inside). Each of these wrapped packages contains a joke, a plastic trinket, and a paper crown. As we eat, we read our jokes to each other, trade trinkets, and laugh at my grandfather's crown, which inevitably sits askew on his head.

Sure, it's not your traditional tradition, but it works for us. It reconnects us with our loved ones and gives us a chance to savor those connections.

When it came time to plan the role of tradition in our wedding, we took a similar approach. We decided to retain the sentiment of traditions but to reimagine their form. Instead of a unity candle, for example, we had our quilt-wrapping ceremony. Our ceremony captured the same sentiment: the unification of families.

For those who already have meaningful rituals and traditions from your religion or heritage, hooray! For those who don't, feel free to create some as you start your new family. Here are a few ideas:

- Exchange gifts. You and your beloved can present each other with surprise gifts during the ceremony, to represent the gift of yourself that you bring to the relationship as well as the thoughtfulness and consideration needed to sustain a relationship on a daily basis. I read about one woman who gave her partner a box of epistolary journal entries she had addressed to him while they were dating; he gave her a pot with dirt from every place he had lived.
- "Warm" the rings. Before the ring exchange, the rings can be passed from guest to guest to be imbued with warm wishes. This idea works best with a small guest list.

AN INTIMATE RITUAL

We never wanted a ceremony. We had been together for eleven years, since high school, and while we knew a wedding was important as a way to include our friends and family in our commitment, it was also something of a nonevent to us. We'd thought of ourselves as married for years and acted that way. We'd gone through lots of good times as well as bad times and had worked through them as a committed couple long before our marriage certificate was signed.

So when it came time to actually plan a wedding, we had a lot of discussions about what we wanted, what might be "expected," and what would be the right fit for the day. We talked about eloping, but we knew it was important to our families and friends to witness our union. We settled on just throwing a celebration without a ceremony, but the closer we got to our wedding day, the more I felt like we needed to do *something* ceremonial. But neither of us was into the whole wedding thing. I don't like being the center of attention; neither of us is remotely religious; and after eleven years together, it didn't seem important to say vows—we'd been saying them in the way we took care of each other for years.

So we decided to mush together a bunch of customs I'd read about and have a wrist binding. We included a note with the invitation explaining that there would not be a traditional ceremony (I didn't want people coming with expectations) and inviting people to bring their own string to help us literally "tie the knot." This wouldn't be part of a structured ceremony (like a handfasting) but instead would be a chance for people to have time with us as a couple during the first hour of the evening.

I can't tell you how much I worried about this. It was exactly what I wanted to do, but I was afraid people would think it was too weird and that it would wind up feeling silly instead of meaningful. But when Jeff's grandpa tied the first string onto our wrists—a piece of ribbon saved from the cake at the fiftieth anniversary of his wedding to Jeff's (now deceased) grandmother—I knew we had made the right choice. Some people brought store-bought ribbons, and some used ribbons from the large stash we provided, but an amazing number of guests brought sentimental pieces: ribbons from their own wedding gifts or favors; a piece of lace from a pillowcase made by Jeff's other (also passed) grandmother; yarn they had spun themselves.

The whole thing was an incredibly affirming experience. It let our guests spend some time with us outside of a receiving line (where you know someone's always waiting to be next, right behind you). It opened people up—they told us about their weddings or their wishes for us. It made each guest a part of the wedding, which was really important because a lot of this wedding was for the guests, not for me. And it made us feel like each guest was affirming our choice to be together. We knew we had a huge network of love and support. And the best part was that we were physically tied together for an hour. Often, the bride and groom rarely see each other on their wedding day. Well, we were stuck with each other, which meant that we both heard all the wonderful stories and we gave an awful lot of three-armed hugs.

—Liz Grotyohann

- Encourage guests to greet each other. At some point before, during, or after the ceremony, guests can be encouraged to introduce themselves to someone they don't know. This practice can help build the community that will support your marriage.
- Invite guests to speak. A modification of the traditional Quaker meeting is to set aside about ten minutes to encourage guests to stand and speak if they are moved to do so. Guests might recite poems or state their wishes for you. Giving guests advance notice about this element of the ceremony will provide them with a chance to collect their thoughts (and their courage).
- Collect messages from guests. As guests arrive, pass out small pieces of paper and ask them to write well wishes, advice, or hopes for the couple. At some point during the ceremony, pass around a vase to collect the messages.
- Pour unity sand. Instead of lighting candles to symbolize unity, pour different colors of sand to represent the merging of families but to honor the continued presence of the individual. (The sands will mix, but each color will still be clearly seen.)

AVOIDING THE SPOTLIGHT

The general assumption at weddings is that the couple is the center of attention and that they like it. While this is true for lots of couples, it's not true for everyone. If it's not true for you, elopement is not your only choice. You have options. You could consider:

- Having the ceremony in private and then partying with your friends and family afterward.
- Forgoing one large wedding and instead holding small receptions at different places around the country, depending on where your friends and family are concentrated.
- Not using a microphone during your ceremony. (As a guest, I get frustrated when I can't hear what the couple is saying, but it's your wedding, and you should do what you want.)
- Wearing casual clothing.
- Skipping things like the grand entrance, the first dance, the bouquet toss, and the garter thing. Instead, treat your wedding more like a regular party.

If you find yourselves feeling anxious or uncomfortable about any part of the wedding, figure out how to eliminate or modify it. There are no rules!

CEREMONY FLOWERS

One reason Matt and I chose to get married outside was to let nature do the decorating. (But even if we had gotten married inside, we still would have gone bare bones to save money and lessen our impact on the environment.) We asked a good friend to collect wildflowers on the day of the wedding and to fashion them into a bouquet using ribbon and string from our craft closet. I made flower pins for everyone in the wedding party using scraps of fabric left over from my dress sash and Matt's tie.

Molly and her partner, Aaron, also took a minimalist approach to ceremony flowers. They got flowers from a local flower shop and had Molly's mom arrange them and bind them with a white ribbon. They purchased a single lily for each bridesmaid and "snips of goldenrod" for the groomsmen to wear as boutonnieres.

HOW TO DIY YOUR FLOWERS

I loved the idea of having lots of flowers at our ceremony and reception but did not want to pay outrageous prices for floral arrangements. After looking through countless images on the Internet, I decided to buy white and green chrysanthemums wholesale from Whole Blossom (which I definitely recommend, since the merchandise is verified organic, sustainable, and beautiful) and baby's breath from a local grocery store.

Having an outdoor wedding with colors of ivory, green, and brown, I decided that delicate bouquets of baby's breath would be perfect for the bridesmaids. The remainder of the flowers, including the bridal bouquet, reception centerpieces, ring bearer pillow, and boutonnieres, would be white and green chrysanthemums.

I asked the bridesmaids to help make bouquets after the rehearsal. I wanted the experience to be relaxed and memorable. I wanted us to spend time together before the hustle and bustle of the wedding day. Thankfully, they were all pretty excited about the idea.

The night before the wedding, the bridesmaids, along with friends staying with us, circled around five-gallon buckets filled with flowers. I showed them how to tie about twenty stems of baby's breath for the bouquets and how to use a mix of green and white button mums nestled in a few pieces of fern leaves to make boutonnieres. From there, their creativity took off! We all played around with flowers, and I asked for suggestions on what they thought looked and worked best.

—Christa Howard

Emily and her partner, Greg, wanted flowers to decorate their ceremony site, but they wanted to be as eco-friendly as possible. They bought live, potted, organic gaillardia, which they put in galvanized buckets and hung by the seats. After the ceremony, the flowers served as centerpieces at the reception. Emily says, "After the wedding, the flowers were split up between various family members and planted in our yard, our parents' yards, and [the yards of] some extended family and are living reminders of that wonderful weekend."

As with any wedding decision, you have to do what feels right to you. It can help to apply the 10-10-10 Rule to prioritize flowers properly. How will you feel about your approach to flowers in ten minutes? Ten months? Ten years? Some other ideas for ceremony flowers:

- Get them from someone's yard. I'm not talking about stealing, of course. I'm talking about finding people who grow beautiful flowers in their backyard (in your neighborhood or your town) and asking if they would be willing to donate them to your wedding. The right people might be flattered to have their work showcased in your wedding.
- Make them (or buy them handmade). Consider flowers made out of paper, yarn, or fabric.
- Replace them. Instead of flowers, why not use potted herbs? Pinwheels? Old-fashioned lollipops?
- Grow your own. If you've been meaning to take up a new hobby such as gardening, now might be the perfect opportunity to learn and to produce something for your wedding.

CEREMONY MUSIC

Do you want music playing before, during, or after your ceremony? Matt and I wanted music because we love it, because we thought it would relax us, and because we wanted the whole event to feel like a party. But we also wanted the setup to be as stress-free as possible. Since we'd already decided to have a microphone system that included a speaker, we made a preceremony playlist on our iPod and put someone in charge of turning it on and off. We played nontraditional artists we like, such as Jens Lekman. His song "Your Arms Around Me" gets to the heart of what marriage is for us. (It's about going to the emergency room after getting injured while slicing an avocado. You know—life.) Other music options include an MP3 player attached to speakers and live instrumentalists or singers.

CEREMONY PROGRAMS

I haven't kept a single program from the ten-plus weddings I've been to, so maybe I'm biased. I tend to think that wedding programs are one of those "traditions" invented by the wedding industrial complex to get couples to spend more money. Some good friends of ours chose not to have ceremony programs, and I didn't even notice until the wedding was over.

All that being said, Matt and I decided to create wedding programs for two reasons. First, our ceremony was very nontraditional. We thought our more traditional friends and family might feel comfortable if they could at least follow along and have a sense of where the ceremony was going. Second, I'm a very visual learner, and I like to read key points during oral presentations. We also included a lot of quotes that we thought people might want to reread. Finally, we included information about the nontraditional reception to help people wrap their minds around it. We pointed out where the recycling bin was after the ceremony and gave people permission to unload the programs right away.

In the end, I'm glad we had ceremony programs, but they weren't essential. If we had gotten married inside, I would have preferred a more environmentally friendly way of sharing the same information, perhaps with an LCD projector and a blank wall.

You can choose to have printed programs, handwritten cards, or no program at all. It's up to you.

ALTERNATIVES TO RING PILLOWS

Matt and I saved ourselves a lot of grief by ignoring the traditional "things you must buy to make your wedding special" list: no aisle runners, ceremony decorations, cake toppers, guestbook, cake-cutting knife. We would have put a ring pillow on that list, except that Matt's grandma randomly sent us the hat she wore in her wedding. I wasn't planning on wearing a hat during the ceremony, and it didn't match my dress, so we decided to turn it into a ring pillow. I used buttons to attach a ribbon to the hat. Then tied the rings to the ribbon. Voila!

Other ideas for carrying your rings:

- Use a ribbon to attach the ring to your wrist—a very intimate and personal touch.
- Attach the ring to your favorite book by tying a ribbon or string around it.
- Tie the rings to a potted plant.
- Carry them in a vintage bowl (which you can display in your home later, as a reminder of your wedding).
- Carry them in the jewelry boxes they came in.

- Make your own ring pillow. Pillows are simple projects, even for beginning sewers and even without a sewing machine.
- Other: ______________________________

If you have an heirloom that you want to incorporate into the ring ceremony, absolutely go for it. If making your own ring pillow (see "DIY Project 7" page 129) will help you slow down and ponder the commitment you are about to enter, satiate your need for creativity, or fill you with a sense of accomplishment, then by all means do it. But if you start to feel stress about the ring pillow or spending money you don't have to purchase something you don't need, feel free to drop the whole thing. Pockets work just as well.

IDEAS FOR NEXT STEPS

- Work with your partner to complete the ceremony vision worksheet. Starting with the big picture can help you stay focused on your goals rather than getting overwhelmed by the details.
- If you are writing your own ceremony script, create a draft. Swing by http://2000dollarwedding.com/p/ceremony-scripts.html for inspiration from likeminded couples. If your officiant is writing the script, start the collaboration and discussion earlier rather than later.
- Remember that while the words matter, *love* is a verb. Your day-to-day actions matter more than words.
- Make a plan for flowers (or no flowers) at your ceremony.
- Decide whether or not to have music at your ceremony.
- Decide whether or not to have ceremony programs.
- Have fun!

DIY Project 4:

BOUTONNIERE

This simple DIY boutonniere idea came from my friend's wedding. I had so much fun sitting around talking, laughing, and crafting these boutonnieres the night before her wedding. The bride's relaxed expectations and attitude about the whole process made the experience even more fun. This project illustrates that DIY can be easy, inexpensive, *and* elegant.

MATERIALS

Scissors (preferably sharp sewing scissors)
Small flowers of your choice (such as mums)
Plants of your choice (such as ferns)
Floral tape
A straight pin

DIRECTIONS

1. Arrange two to four flowers with small stems in front of a couple of plant leave tips.
2. Tightly wrap the stems with floral tape.
3. Use a straight pin to attach the boutonniere.

Tip: *Try different flowers and plants to create unique combinations.*

Jill + Sam
Saturday · July 11 · 2011 · Los Angeles, CA
Birds of a Feather
"Hope is the thing with feathers
That perches in the soul,
And sings the tune without the words,
And never stops at all." —Emily Dickinson
officiant | Andy Dehnart, Sara's best friend from Stetson University and Matt's good friend
Wedding party | (from left to right)
Caroline Diggins, Matt's friend from Indiana University
Brian Crabill, Matt's friend from Ultimate Frisbee in college
John Bradford, Matt's youngest brother
Mike Bradford, Matt's oldest brother
Brent Maddin, Sara's friend from Teach For America in rural Louisiana
Jamie Dillemuth, Sara's friend from KIPP Academy in Houston
Camella Clements, Sara's friend from KIPP Academy in Houston
Chong Hao-Fu, Sara's friend from KIPP Academy in Houston
Reception | Sunshine Mountain Lodge
• Located six miles south on the right-hand side of Highway 7.
• Please park on the shoulder of the road.
• Feel free to change into more comfortable clothes or come as you are, and bring your bathing suits if you want to go in the hot tub.
• Dinner will be buffet style. Appetizers (starting immediately): chips and salsa, guacamole, seven-layer dip. Main Course (starting around 6pm): vegetarian/chicken/beef fajitas, tamales, make-your-own quesadillas. Side: black bean corn salad. Dessert (around 8:15): Cake (vanilla berry, cheesecake, tiramisu, carrot). Drinks: beer, wine, frozen strawberry margaritas, soda, juice.
• Have fun with board games, the campfire, dancing on the patio, a walk in the woods, the video of Matt and Sara, etc. Dancing will start around 8:45 p.m.
• Make yourself at home!

DIY Project 5:

CEREMONY PROGRAM FANS

These ceremony program fans are perfect for summer outdoor weddings. They display information about your ceremony in a functional and beautiful way.

MATERIALS

Cardstock (in a color that shows type legibly and in a thickness that can feed through your printer)

A paper cutter, scissors, or craft knife

Spray adhesive

Wavy fan handles (you can find these on the Internet, by doing a quick search)

Optional: corner rounder

DIRECTIONS

1. Use a word processing or design program such as InDesign to make the program. We changed the orientation of the paper, so that the front was in the left column and the back was in the right column. That way, each program required only one sheet of cardstock. You can download our template at http://2000dollarwedding.com/p/project-templates.html.
2. Print your programs on thick cardstock. You might want to print a few extra just in case.
3. Use a paper cutter, scissors, or a craft knife to cut each piece of cardstock into a front side and a back side. Paper cutters typically have a ruler to allow you to measure your cuts precisely.
4. Prepare an area for using the spray adhesive, preferably on the outside. Lay down a protective surface to cover the ground, since spray adhesive is difficult to contain.
5. Spray the back of one side of each card and sandwich a wavy fan handle between the front and back, matching the sides as carefully as possible.
6. When the glue dries, trim around the edges with scissors to remove any areas that don't match up.
7. Round the corners with a corner rounder (optional).

Tips

- You can make the fans any size you want, but the bigger they are, the floppier they will be.
- If your printer starts smearing your cards, wait a few minutes before printing the next one.
- Consider tying a piece of ribbon to the base of each program.
- Get fancy by putting an interactive game about you and your partner, such as a crossword puzzle or Mad Libs, on the back. Drill a small hole through the wavy fan handle and thread a golf pencil on a ribbon through the hole.

Matt-n-Sara
of a feather
7.19.08

DIY Project 6:

WEDDING QUILT DUVET COVER

A quilt is a wonderful heirloom that will remind you of your wedding for years to come. You can ask guests to send meaningful fabric scraps in advance, use iron-transfer photo paper to make quilt squares out of photographs, or recycle childhood T-shirts. The quilt could be used during the ceremony or put on display during the reception. You could also ask guests to use fabric paint to decorate squares during your wedding and turn them into a quilt afterward. Only basic sewing skills are required for this project.

MATERIALS

Fabric for the quilt squares
Fabric for the background around the squares
A bed sheet for the back of your duvet cover
Buttons to close the bottom of your duvet cover
A blanket to fit inside your duvet cover
Thread
Scissors (preferably sharp sewing scissors)

Tip: With a few extra steps, you can easily turn this into a real quilt instead of a duvet cover. Let the Internet be your trusty guide.

DIRECTIONS

1. Decide how big your quilted duvet cover will be, based on how big the blanket you want to cover is. Figure out the approximate width and height, how many squares will be in each row, how big the squares will be, and how far apart they will be spaced.
2. Draw a sketch of your quilt, including dimensions.
3. Draw a sketch of the pattern for each individual square. Don't worry about the exact size of each piece of fabric. Just figure out which piece you are going to sew first, second, third, and so on.
4. To make each square, cut a smaller square for the very center. The size doesn't matter, but it shouldn't be so small that it's difficult to sew other pieces to it and it shouldn't be so large that you don't have room for additional pieces.
5. Cut a rectangular piece that is the same length as the square in the center. Place the square and the rectangle right sides together along one edge and sew along the edge (backstitching at the end of each line to ensure durability).

continued →

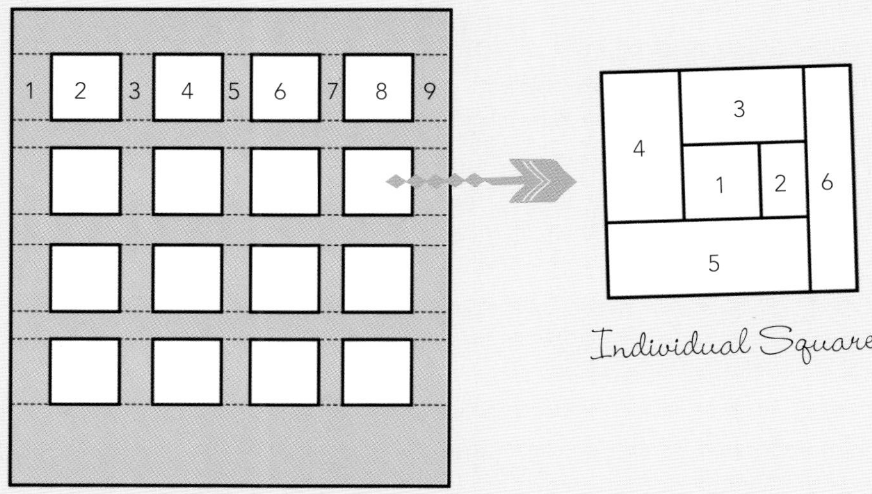

6. Unfold the fabric, press the seam open to each side with your fingers, and iron the seam open flat.
7. Stop and pat yourself on the back. You're quilting!
8. Cut another piece of fabric the length of the first piece and the second piece put together. Place the square, the rectangle, and the new rectangle right sides together along one edge and sew along the edge (backstitching at each end of the line to ensure durability).
9. Unfold the fabric, press the seam open to each side with your fingers, and iron the seam open flat.
10. Continue this process of radiating around the center square until the quilt square reaches your desired size for an individual square.
11. Now it's time to quilt the squares to another type of fabric to make long strips. The process is the same: Match right side to right side, sew, and press open. You'll sew one piece of contrasting fabric to a quilt square and another piece of contrasting fabric to the other side (always placing right sides together). Continue until you have sewn a horizontal strip.
12. Quilt your long horizontal together with long strips of contrasting fabrics, following the same process: right side of the fabric to right side, sew, and press open.
13. To finish the project, place your quilt top right side to right side with the sheet, with the finished edge of the sheet at the bottom of the quilt. Sew around three sides, leaving the bottom open. Add buttons and buttonholes to close the bottom. If your sewing machine doesn't automatically create buttonholes, consider another closure option, such as snaps or Velcro.

DIY Project 7:

RING PILLOW

Making your own ring pillow is an excellent first sewing project to strengthen your skills and confidence. If you're already a seamstress (or somewhere in between), this project will be simple and satisfying.

MATERIALS

Two pieces of fabric for the top and bottom of your pillow
Stuffing (try recycling a secondhand throw pillow)
A coordinating button
Coordinating ribbon
Thread
Scissors (preferably sharp sewing scissors)

DIRECTIONS

1. Decide on the final length and height of your ring pillow. (The sample is approximately 5x5 inches.)
2. Add approximately ¾ inch all the way around for your seam allowance (the area that will be cut off when you sew the front and back together) and for a little poof from the stuffing.
3. Following the dimensions you just determined, cut a square for the front and the back at the same time. If you are using the same piece of fabric, fold it right side to right side (in other words, fold the front of the fabric on one piece to the front of the fabric on the other piece). If you are using two different fabrics for the top and bottom of your pillow, also match them right side to right side. Cut out the two pieces simultaneously so they will be the exact same size and shape.
4. Keeping the right sides matched up, sew around three of the four sides.
5. On the fourth side, leave a hole big enough for the stuffing but small enough to sew by hand.
6. Turn the fabric inside out so that the proper side is now on the outside.
7. Use a pencil to poke the corners out straight.
8. Stuff your ring pillow to the desired thickness.
9. Sew the small hole closed by hand.
10. Cut a length of ribbon long enough to hold the rings, to be tied in the position you want.
11. Sew a button on top of the ribbon, into the middle of the pillow.

Tips

- You can embroider the fabric before sewing it, stamp plain fabric with paint, make a felt flower for the center of your pillow, wrap the ribbon around the pillow like a present, or try different fabrics such as burlap or vintage handkerchiefs.
- Instead of making a tiny pillow, make a throw pillow, to have a frequent reminder of your wedding lying around the house.
- If you make a sewing mistake at any point in the process, just whip out your trusty seam ripper, take apart the stitching, and try again.

ON THE BODY: Attire, Hair, Makeup, and Rings

Now that we've focused on the ceremony, we can move along to details related to the body, such as rings, wedding attire (including what to do with it after the wedding), hair, and makeup. We will also talk about options for dressing the wedding party. The DIY project for this chapter gives directions for making your own tie. This section starts with Matt's and my story about how we handled everything related to these details. It ends with specific ideas for next steps.

OUR STORY

Rings are one of those wedding traditions Matt and I said "I do" to because we like the symbolism of them—unity and no end. However, we didn't like their history. We were disturbed by the diamond trade and the effect that mining has on the environment. I conducted an intense Internet search to find vintage rings but had trouble finding something simple and practical enough to fit my lifestyle. Next, we turned to pawn shops, but we had trouble getting past all the possible situations that lead people to sell their intimate belongings.

Finally, we turned to environmentally friendly jewelry companies. We came across a company called greenKarat that appealed to our eco-friendliness and budget-mindedness. The company set up a registry for friends and family to donate old gold, which was then melted and cast into new rings. It gave us credit for each ounce of donated gold and applied it toward the purchase of our rings.

Again we tapped into our guest e-mail list. We reminded everyone to RSVP for the wedding and asked them to donate any old gold they had lying around the house (breakup jewelry, broken chains, one earring, and so on). We assuaged people's fears by telling them that any bad karma would be melted away in the process. Eleven friends and family members came through and donated more than $1,000 in gold, which brought our total for two rings down to $109.

I seriously considered going with moissanite, a synthetic gem very close to diamond (although it's cheaper and better for the environment than mined diamond), but in the end chose an orange synthetic sapphire. As far as design goes, I knew I wanted something practical. I'm not an experienced jewelry wearer, and I was nervous about wearing a ring every day for the rest of my life. I wanted something that would enhance rather than interfere with my life. I didn't want to have to take off my ring to cook, clean, shower, or exercise. I wanted a ring for life—my day-to-day life.

I chose a very simple band with a very small (2mm) stone. It provides a little sparkle, but it's small enough not to get caught on anything, and it doesn't leave indentions in my face when I lean on it. It's also baby friendly. I don't have to worry about scratching a cheek.

Although I felt a lot of insecurity and self-doubt about my unconventional ring choice, I kept reminding myself that it was the option that made the most sense for me and my lifestyle. I wasn't wearing the ring to impress people or gather compliments Why did it matter what other people thought about it? I've finally come to a very happy place with my ring. It fits effortlessly into my life. It's a constant reminder and symbol of our wedding and marriage—on our own terms.

We took a similarly unconventional route when it came to buying a wedding dress. I requested that 10 percent of our budget go toward my dress. At the time, $200 seemed like a perfectly reasonable amount to spend on a wedding dress.

I wanted to feel good in my choice. I knew that the more I liked the dress, the more comfortable I would feel. That said, I was eager to spend less money if possible. I felt insecure about our ability to stay within our meager budget.

Although I very much appreciate nonwhite wedding dresses because of their postwedding practicality, I felt compelled to find a white dress for my own wedding. I think I worried about freaking out our families. The fact that we were getting married by a lake instead of in a church was already likely to cause consternation and disapproval. To add fuel to the bonfire, a nonclergyman was performing the ceremony. And we were cooking the reception food ourselves. And we sent postcards as invitations. As stupid as it sounds in retrospect, I felt as if I needed to wear a white dress to remind people, "Yes, this is a *real* wedding."

I thought about buying a used wedding dress from Craigslist or eBay or going to the online Target store and buying one at a budget price. I also searched for eco-friendly dresses, which typically cost more than five times my wedding dress budget. I loved the idea of a vintage dress, but I couldn't find anything that fit my body or my style.

Then it occurred to me that I should start looking for sundresses. White is a popular color for sundresses, and a sundress would be appropriate for an outdoor summer wedding. I found myself back at the online Target, staring at a $15 sundress. It was a 1950s-style dress with a V-neck, high waist, and lots of fabric jutting out all around. I was slightly worried that even the waiflike model looked a little big in the dress. If that weren't enough to discourage me, the customer reviews were terrible. Some reviewers called the dress a "potato sack." Others complained that it made them look huge. The dress's only positive, aside from the price, seemed to be that it had plenty of material to prevent it from being see-through.

The dress was an example of my values being at odds with each other. Because it was manufactured by a major discount retailer, the price was amazingly low. However, that same low price was potentially the result of questionable labor policies in developing nations. (Then again, expensive, mass-manufactured clothing is also often the result of questionable labor policies in developing nations.)

I decided to order the dress, even though I never had a "This is the one!" moment. A few days later, my wedding dress arrived in a small box. I giggled because it had pockets and was machine washable. Although the dress didn't look like a potato sack on me, it did make me look—in Matt's words—"bigger than usual." In the end, I decided to keep the dress. I was tired of scouring the Internet and relieved to find something for only $15. My rational side kicked in and reminded me that I didn't need the most perfect dress to have a meaningful and memorable wedding.

I made myself feel better about the dress by committing to making a sash to rein in some of the extra fabric. I found some pinkish-orange cloth in our fabric bin that I had purchased while traveling in India and decided to use it to make the sash. Fortunately, I had also purchased a shawl in India that would coordinate nicely with the sash if I got cold in the evening. My most comfortable pair of high-heeled Dansko shoes are silver, so they coordinated nicely as well. I had a necklace that would look just fine with the dress, thereby completing the ensemble for a whopping $15 (plus tax and shipping).

I further made myself feel better by reveling in the fact that the dress was incredibly comfortable. I could move, walk, sit, and even dance as if I were wearing everyday clothes. I could even wear a normal bra. Because one of our goals was to be relaxed and fully present during our wedding, comfort was important to me. I didn't want to have a nagging voice in the back of my head all evening: "Don't step backward onto your dress. You'll fall!"

Finally, I made myself feel better about the dress by asking one of my colleagues (a seamstress) to alter the high, rounded back into a sexier V shape. She graciously agreed, and Matt and I had a fun evening at her house with pizza and salad. Matt fixed her computer while she fixed my dress.

Although the back looked lovely when she was done, I was concerned that I looked a bit frumpy. I stared into a full-length mirror and had to squash the tears that threatened to erupt down my cheeks.

I told myself that I could continue looking for a dress if I *really* wanted to. Then Matt and I decided to add an embroidered design to the bottom, and I finally started to get excited. A few months earlier, I had taught myself to embroider from a book and had successfully cranked out a dishtowel (of which only a small corner was embroidered). That project had taken an entire day to complete. But we still had five months until the wedding. I was optimistic that I could embroider all 100 inches of fabric along the bottom of the dress.

Matt suggested that we embroider the story of our lives together. Going along with our de facto bird theme, we drew several scenes with ourselves as birds. For example, on our first date, we had run through sprinklers at a local elementary school. For the dress, we drew two birds splashing around in a birdbath. In the five months before the wedding, every time I had a phone conversation with a friend or a family member, I grabbed the dress and embroidered. Other times I embroidered alone for a meditative effect. I have such special memories of working on the embroidery, thinking about weddings and marriage, and feeling proud of my accomplishments.

In retrospect, I'm thankful that I didn't get too stressed or crazy about the dress. My goal was to be comfortable, feel confident, and make my dress special with sincerity rather than with money. Even though it wasn't the perfect dress, it did meet those expectations.

I decided to stay pretty low-key about hair and makeup too. Because they weren't a priority, we didn't allocate any money toward them in the budget. I begged a friend to do my hair and decided to do my makeup myself.

My friend and I planned to rehearse my hairdo the night before the wedding, but I didn't want to pull myself away from the welcome picnic to make time for that. So we didn't rehearse, and my hair turned out just fine. Late in the evening, when it started to get loose and fall down, I took out all the bobby pins, twisted my hair up off my neck and out of my face, and clipped my day-to-day barrette in. I was too busy having fun to care about how my hair looked.

RINGS

Finding the right rings (if you want rings; you could also have tattoos or nothing at all!) is a balancing act, like so many other decisions. There's a lot to juggle: eco-friendliness, cost, aesthetics, comfort, and practicality.

Erin, a mental health therapist from Pittsburgh, said, "My partner works with refugees in Africa, and we both have devoted much of our work to social justice issues, so we never thought of a diamond. There were no rings when he proposed, but we each wound up with an engagement ring (why do only women have them?): his made from a seed in Puerto Rico (where we got engaged), and mine was my great-grandmother's engagement ring, which was so special and meaningful to wear every day." They custom-ordered wedding bands on Etsy.com from an artist who works with fair-trade silver. Erin said the bands were "affordable and uniquely ours, with a lot of personal attention from the lovely artist."

On the other hand, Amy and her partner, Keith, picked out their rings at a typical jewelry store. Similarly, Rachel decided that she "wanted a bit of bling." But she "didn't want a natural (read: conflict) diamond." So they "found a company (bonus, they're local!) that does lab-created diamonds at an amazing price. They also source most of their gold from Canada or reclamation, so it's as 'green' as possible."

Ways of finding rings that suit you and your partner include:

- Asking family members about an heirloom you might be able to have
- Scouring pawn shops
- Looking into environmentally friendly ring companies
- Browsing handcrafted rings (like those found on Etsy.com)
- Connecting with companies that specialize in affordable rings (such as TurtleLoveCommittee.com)

- Looking into alternative metals, such as tungsten, a popular option for a light and durable ring
- Seeking out local artisans to make custom designs (design your own or ask the artist for input)
- Other Ideas: ______________________________

As you think through each option and try to balance it against your values and desires, you might find the following chart useful. Enter your top options in the left-hand column. As you evaluate each option according to the criteria across the top, give it a rating of 1 to 5, with 1 being the lowest and 5 being the highest.

Wedding Ring Matrix

Option	Cost	Aesthetic Appeal	Eco-friendliness	Durability	Practicality
Total					

GETTING IN SHAPE

"How to have a wedding waist in five days." That was the kind of scary advertisement that showed up in the sidebars of my e-mail inbox for the entire seven months we planned our wedding. This topic is such a sensitive one. It's difficult to talk about without somehow reinforcing unrealistic and cruel social expectations about women's bodies. My intent is not to play into those expectations at all. I just want to insert my two cents into the dialogue by saying that if your wedding motivates you to change your eating and exercise patterns, make sure you think about it as a lifestyle change rather than a diet.

A lot of women become obsessed with losing weight, toning, and sculpting their bodies for the "biggest day of their lives." One problem with so many of these discussions is that losing weight is not the same thing as being healthy. Plus, obtaining a healthy body through healthy eating and exercise is a process, not a product. It's about changing your lifestyles, not dieting. In other words, it's not about the wedding; it's about being healthy for a lifetime of marriage.

If you lose weight just for your wedding, you're likely to put it back on once the big event comes and goes. There's even a phenomenon called the Newlywed Nine (pounds). That's how ubiquitous the problem is.

If your wedding motivates you to adopt a healthier lifestyle, that's great! Sometimes external motivation can be helpful. But please don't think of the change as a diet. If you deprive yourself to lose weight for your wedding day, then you're likely to start rewarding yourself once your wedding is over, leading to weight gain. Instead, think about changing your lifestyle—till death do you part. If you're already happy with your current lifestyle with regard to health and wellness, that's even better.

Some tips for a healthier lifestyle:

- Stop thinking of it as a diet. Period. Our culture is very goal-oriented. We set a goal, work hard to achieve it, achieve it, and then move on to a new goal. However, weight loss doesn't work that way. You can't move on to a new goal once you've achieved your ideal weight. You have to maintain it. It's like doing yoga to become flexible. Once you reach your flexibility goal, you have to keep stretching regularly to maintain it. You can't just stop. Similarly, if you return to your pre-goal eating habits, your pre-goal weight will return. Therefore, the goal should not be a number on the scale. The goal should be a healthy lifestyle of eating and exercise that allows you to maintain your ideal body. Start thinking of it as a lifestyle change.
- Make friends with moderation. If you're dieting, you're likely to cut out foods like ice cream, chips, and brownies. If you're making a lifestyle change, you realize that it's much more sustainable to eat such things in

moderation. The goal is to come up with a plan you can sustain for the long haul.

- Expend more calories than you consume. Eating less will cause you to consume fewer calories. Exercising more will cause you to expend more calories. (But exercising does not burn as many calories as you might think. Be careful not to justify eating more simply because you're exercising.) Also, minimize your calories from liquids. Juices, alcoholic beverages, and other drinks are high in calories. As much as possible, stick to water (and get your fruit nutrients from actual fruit, which has much more fiber than juice). Keep a food journal to be honest with yourself about how many calories you are actually eating. Find a healthy friend (or an unhealthy one who is committed to getting healthier) to be your accountability partner. Share your food journal with this person and plan time to exercise together.
- Eat real food. Americans often decrease caloric intake by eating "fake food"—processed food made delicious with fake sweeteners and other unhealthy ingredients. Examples: Diet Coke, fat-free potato chips made with Olestra, margarine—basically, anything labeled as "lite" or "diet." People flock to these foods because they are low in calories. But remember that it's about being healthy, not just about losing weight. And those nutritionally empty foods do have calories. If you eat too many of them, you will gain weight.
- Figure out the underlying causes of your unhealthy lifestyle. Do you eat when you are stressed? Lonely? Confused? Angry? Bored? Pay close attention to your eating habits and try to find substitutes for your unhealthy ones. Do you overeat in social situations because you're nervous? Do you constantly eat unhealthy food because it's more convenient and your job takes up most of your spare time and energy? Again, be honest with yourself about what's going on and figure out strategies for fixing the problem.

THE DRESS (OR OTHER WEDDING OUTFIT)

If you walk into a room full of kindergartners and ask them to draw a wedding, their pictures will probably all include a big, white, puffy dress. Contrary to the image that is burned into our collective mind's eye, there are lots of options for wedding dresses (including big, white, puffy ones!). You could:

- Find a vintage dress. The Internet is chock-full of beautiful vintage finds. Although many of them come with teeny, tiny waists, you might be able to enlarge them, depending on how much extra fabric is included in the

seams. Vintage dresses from estate sales or secondhand shops will cost much less than those from fancy vintage shops. If you can alter a dress yourself or have a friend or family member do it for free, great. Otherwise, factor in the cost of alterations with a trusted seamstress or tailor.

- Buy a used wedding dress. A quick Internet search for "used wedding dresses" will yield dozens of sites that facilitate bride-to-bride selling. Many of the dresses are not even used, since some brides buy more than one dress in the decision phase. Another good place to look is Brides Against Breast Cancer, which holds sales throughout the country, with all proceeds going toward making wishes come true for breast cancer patients.
- Find a seamstress. Often, a little digging will reveal a seamstress among your friends, family, coworkers, neighbors, or church members. I've seen seamstresses re-create designer wedding dresses for significantly less than the original. Seamstresses can also work from vintage patterns to re-create dresses (that actually fit your waist).
- Personalize an inexpensive wedding dress. One of the most beautiful dresses I've ever seen was a $68 dress from Target that the bride used as a blank canvas for gorgeous black appliqué. The possibilities are endless.
- Go with a bridesmaid dress. It's fairly easy to find bridesmaid dresses that resemble wedding dresses, for a fraction of the cost. A lot of bridal shops won't have white or ivory samples in the store, but you can try on another color and then order the color you want (not necessarily white or ivory either).
- Buy a nonwedding dress. You and your fiancé are the ones getting married; it's your wedding. If you want to wear a gorgeous nonwedding dress (or pantsuit, skirt, or bikini for that matter), it's your prerogative. Two of my good friends got married in shorts, and their wedding was very meaningful and memorable. In the past, a woman simply wore her best dress and called it a day. Going the nonwedding dress route can also mean wearing a vast array of funky colors.

Andrea, who works in e-commerce and marketing support in Syracuse, looked "everywhere" with her mom and was "flabbergasted by the prices, especially at David's Bridal, where most of the dresses are polyester (tablecloth type material)." One day, they were walking through Jo-Ann Fabric and Craft "and saw the pattern section. I said, 'Hey, wouldn't it be cool if you made my dress?' At first she was like, 'Absolutely not. I don't know how to make a wedding dress!' But by the end of the store visit, we had purchased a couple of patterns for her to try. It was a very long, kind of nerve-wracking process for her, but in the end I wore something my mother had created and it was an amazing feeling!"

Kristen, an artist and Web developer from California, tried a couple of different strategies to find her dress. She described the process as a nightmare. She started at a bridal boutique that was having a sale and "almost threw up in those dresses." Then she went the David's Bridal route, which wasn't for her either. She "wanted something beautiful but simple (NO TRAIN!)." Finally, "things started getting better when I realized that Nordstrom and Macy's carry much simpler dresses. I would order three at a time online and then return them to my local store. I ended up finding a dress at Macy's I really liked for $150."

In the middle of wedding planning, the dress can feel like the biggest deal imaginable. It can feel like a nonnegotiable—that is, "I must find the Perfect Dress or my wedding won't be complete." You probably care more about your dress than any of your wedding guests do. You're going to look beautiful, no matter what. The guests are going to look at your smile and the brightness in your eyes. They're going to care more about seeing old friends, enjoying good food, and basking in the general happiness of the event. Find a dress (or other outfit) you like, but don't spend too much time pining for things you can't afford.

WHAT TO DO WITH THE DRESS AFTER THE WEDDING

One thing I didn't think about while selecting a dress was what I would do with it once the wedding was over. Here are some options:

- Resell it. This option makes sense for those who choose expensive, fancy dresses. That way, you recoup some of the money you spent. Even better, you can resell a dress that you bought used. Wedding dresses are like cars; they start depreciating as soon as you take them off the lot (except for dresses that will be considered vintage in fifty years, I suppose). The same bride-to-bride selling sites that you can use to find a dress can be used to sell a dress.

- Store it. This option makes sense for people who like to reminisce with artifacts. If you decide to go this route, make sure to research how to properly store the dress to ensure that it doesn't yellow over time. This option can add expense and hassle, but if it's meaningful for you, that's what matters.

- Donate it. Consider creating good karma for your marriage by donating your wedding dress to another bride-to-be and elevating the general happiness level of the world. Brides Against Breast Cancer is an excellent option for the donation route.

MY $68 WEDDING DRESS

I am not a wedding person. Before I met my husband, I had never even entertained the thought of getting married, let alone having a big wedding. If I'd had my way, we would have run off to the woods and gotten married by ourselves and then had a big party afterward. But other people had other (strong) opinions. So a slightly more traditional shindig it was. But I decided to make as many things as possible—from the invitations to the favors to the dress.

Not being a wedding person, I am also definitively not a wedding dress person. I went into a couple of bridal stores but promptly ran out hyperventilating before even looking at anything. After a couple of J.Crew dresses that had to be returned due to total cleavage obscenity, I ordered a cheapo sheath dress from Target. It was so cheapo ($68 on sale) that I really held out no hopes for it. But when it arrived, it fit perfectly and was made of quite decent material. I thought to myself, "If you don't want to be typical, here's your chance to get creative." I quickly ordered a second dress as a backup, just in case my attempts backfired. I mean, the dresses cost $68, for Pete's sake.

After many experiments with cutting into the dress, fabric flowers, paint, and beads, I decided on cutout silhouettes. I went to fabric stores. In the dusty basement of one store, I found some flocked velvet backed with acrylic. There are tons of patterns on the Web that you can trace, but I just took a pair of scissors and went at it. I cut out hundreds of leaves, vines, and animals until I had shapes that looked good. (If I had used regular velvet or another fabric, the edges would have shredded when I cut the thin, delicate shapes.) I then laid the dress on the floor and began arranging the pieces until I got a pattern I liked. Then the hot glue gun came out. (Super Glue also works I discovered later. I was too lazy to even try fabric glue.) I attached a piece of netting to extend the train and glued more trailing leaves down that.

After several weeks of working in the evening, I had my dress. It had birds, deer, mice, our initials, a big fox, and the words we had inscribed in our rings: "It's all true." Meaning that every dream, every fairy tale, every story about dragons, empires, or even true love—it's simply all true.

—Kimi Weart

HOW I DYED MY WEDDING DRESS

OR, HOW MY VERY OWN WEDDING DRESS WENT FROM "I DO" TO "PARTY ON" IN SIX EASY STEPS

STEP 1. Purchase two bottles of liquid RIT dye in black (I intended to take my dress from white to black). Doubling the amount of dye will turn a very light item of clothing darker.

STEP 2. Fill the sink with enough "hot as you can get it" water for the garment to move around freely. Add two bottles of RIT liquid dye before adding the garment. Stir the water and dye mixture thoroughly.

STEP 3. Note that the label of the dress says "dry clean only" and that the bottle of RIT clearly says "not for use on dry clean only fabrics." Think about how you'll probably never wear the dress again if it remains white. Then think about how amazing it would be if this actually worked. Say a tiny prayer (or five) and wet the dress with *hot* water before tossing it into the dye-filled sink.

STEP 4. Freak out a little but press on. Stir constantly (up and down, back and forth) for twenty-five minutes. (You want the water to be piping hot when you start because dyeing works best if the fabric remains in hot water. The hotter the water is to start, the longer you can stir the garment in the dye bath and the longer it will soak up color.)

STEP 5. Remove the item after twenty-five minutes of thorough stirring. Rinse with warm water that gradually gets colder and colder (to seal in the color). Keep rinsing in ice cold water until the water runs clear. After saying a few more prayers, hang the dress up to air dry. (I hung mine in the sunroom with a bucket underneath to catch any drips.)

STEP 6. Thoroughly clean the sink to remove all traces of dye. (This was actually more stressful than dyeing the dress, since dye got everywhere. I was nervous about our stainless sink and granite countertops, but they all came clean with some good old soapy scrubbing.) Sure, my dress ended up a pretty gunmetal-pewter color thanks to the metallic threads that ran through the satin, and not black as I had originally planned. And sure, as my dress dried in the sunroom, it looked totally ruined (and not at all consistent in color). But once it was dry, the color was locked in (no black dye bleeding into my skin as I had worried), and for $12 in dye, I had turned my once-in-a-lifetime gown into a cocktail dress that I can wear time and time again. (And believe me, I'll wear it, as long as I can squeeze into it!)

I realize that this entire process could just as easily have ended in disaster, so I guess the lesson is to only dye something that you might never wear again and remember to stir, stir, stir and use hot, hot, hot water.

Happy dyeing!

—Sherry Petersik, younghouselove.com

- Wear it. I love it when brides purchase dresses they can repurpose for other occasions, although I realize and respect that the idea makes some brides uncomfortable. My good friend Camella had a dress made by a local designer that she can wear to a variety of events. You could also dye your wedding dress, although some bridal fabrics are not amenable to dye. Research before you start dyeing.
- Transform it. I think it's cool to transform your wedding dress into something else you will use on a daily, weekly, or monthly basis (a quilt, throw pillow, bag, curtains). You get the benefit of keeping the memory around but interact with the dress in a more practical, everyday way.

Elizabeth, an office assistant from Ohio, plans to transform her wedding dress. She said, "If we are blessed with any daughters, I do not in any way expect her/them to want my old dress—it will totally be out of fashion by then. I am sure of it. So instead I plan to have the fabric used to make a christening dress for our future children. I think it will be special to have them enter the church in the dress I wore to marry their father."

Sebrina, a graphic designer from Texas, did a "Trash the Dress photo shoot with paint in front of a mural" a couple months after her wedding. Since her dress had a fitted bodice attached to a ball gown skirt, she "cut the skirt part off and turned the bodice into a tie-dyed party blouse." She plans to "use the fabric and netting from the skirt to create a piece of wall art" for her home.

HAIR AND MAKEUP

Figuring out what to do about your hair and makeup could easily turn into another point of stress. Please don't let it! I'm not saying you shouldn't care about hair and makeup or that you shouldn't make a plan for them. I'm just reminding you that they're not going to make or break your wedding.

Ariel Meadow Stallings, the brilliant mind behind the book and blog *Offbeat Bride*, writes about the Smidge Above Rule. She says, "The way I see it, bridal beauty preparations should, at the most, be only a smidge more than your typical beauty routine." The reason this idea resonates with me is twofold. One: I've seen too many people get way too stressed out about their hair and makeup. If you're going only a "smidge above" your normal routine, you're less likely to get too worked up. Two: I've seen too many people go overboard to the point where they don't look like themselves. Strike a compromise between what helps the photos look good and your regular look, whatever that may be.

I can understand why you would want to have your hair and makeup professionally done for your wedding. If that's the case and it fits in your budget, go for it. I'm not advocating against professional hair and makeup. I'm advocating against elevating these small details to a higher level of importance than they deserve. Less stress equals a happier bride—beautiful from the inside out!

DRESSING THE WEDDING PARTY

While we decided to have a wedding party stand next to us, we deviated from tradition by having mixed-gender attendants on both sides. Half of my closest friends are male, and one of Matt's best friends is female. We didn't want to ask the attendants to purchase matching attire. They were giving their time and money to attend our wedding. We couldn't ask them to pay for plane tickets, lodging, rental cars, *and* new outfits they may or may not ever wear again. Further, it just wasn't that important to us. It felt more like an issue of aesthetics.

Instead, we decided to make everyone a flower pin, using a tutorial I found on the Internet. We sent everyone a picture of the flower and asked them to wear clothing that coordinated with the colors in the pin. It worked for the most part, aside from the friend who decided to wear a blue-and-black-striped dress with red sunglasses. Honestly, it didn't matter to us. Our friends looked like themselves, and we were happy to have our wedding pictures capture that.

For those who prefer a more polished (matching) look but still want to give the wedding party some freedom, consider letting attendants select their own styles within a specific shade of a specific color. Or you could specify a general color and let people select their own shades.

Do what makes the most sense for you and your wedding party, but definitely try to apply the 10-10-10 Rule. How much will the decision matter in ten minutes? Ten months? Ten years?

IDEAS FOR NEXT STEPS

- Think about what you want to wear on your wedding day. The choice is yours. No type of clothing is off-limits (a kilt, a traditional dress, a flapper costume). No color is out of bounds. There may be a few who don't like your choice, but they will love you nonetheless (or perhaps they shouldn't be at your wedding).
- Plan what you're going to do with your clothing after the wedding. Will you be able to wear it again? Do you want to store it? Dye it? Resell it?
- Make a plan for hair and makeup, referring to the Smidge Above Rule.
- Decide how to dress the wedding party (if you have a wedding party). Communicate your plan.
- Have fun and remember not to stress too much about your outward appearance. The more joyful, calm, and content you are, the more beautiful you will be.

DIY Project 8:

MAKING A TIE

One of the benefits of DIY is that you sometimes surprise yourself. That's what happened when I made Matt a tie for our wedding. I was shocked to realize that I could actually craft a tie with my own two hands using material from an old dress. The joy! This project has a special place in my heart because it helped make our wedding special with sincerity and heart rather than with money.

MATERIALS

Fabric for the tie
An old tie that you're comfortable taking apart
A seam ripper
Pins
Thread
A needle
An iron and ironing board

DIRECTIONS

1. Use a seam ripper to take apart the old tie, paying close attention to how it was originally put together.
2. Carefully iron out the original material.
3. Place the old material on top of the new material and pin it in place as a pattern, including the two triangles at each end of the tie.
4. Carefully cut around the tie.
5. Sew each triangle to each end of the tie by sewing the right side of the fabric to the right side.
6. Turn the triangles inside out so that the tie is in the proper direction.
7. Poke a pencil into the corners to push them out as far as they will go.
8. Put the original inner-tie felt piece into the new material.
9. Fold the fabric up around the sides, exactly how it was in the original tie.
10. Pin the tie to secure it in place.
11. Use a slip stitch to sew the tie back up (watching an Internet tutorial if necessary).

Tip: Pick fabrics that are easy to work with. For example, the more slippery the fabric, the more difficult it will be.

THE DETAILS: Food, Flowers, Music, and Photography

Our discussion of details continues with an overview of catering, dessert, and alcohol options (with a philosophical preface about the importance of building good relationships with vendors). We continue the conversation by addressing tableware, centerpieces, and venue decorations and then shift gears to discuss photography and videography (as well as capturing media from guests).

Other details include reception music, how to deejay your own wedding with an iPod, wedding favors, entertaining kids, and how to make seed packets for wedding favors. This section starts with Matt's and my story about how we handled everything related to these details, and it ends with specific ideas for next steps.

OUR STORY

As if it weren't already challenging enough to plan a Saturday ceremony and reception for eighty people with a $2,000 budget, Matt and I made it harder for ourselves by opting to throw a welcome picnic for all our guests on Friday. If our friends and family were going to the trouble of traveling to Colorado for our wedding, we wanted to spend time with them.

Hosting a welcome picnic meant that we not only had to cater a big meal for the reception; we also had to cater a meal for the evening before. We thought through (and rejected) a couple of different options:

- Make-your-own pizza. Matt and I love hosting parties where our guests make their own pizzas. It's so simple and fun! We just chop up a bunch of different toppings, set out the sauce and cheese, and provide small ready-made crusts. Although we loved this idea, we ultimately rejected it because we didn't think some of our elderly guests would be comfortable making their own food.

- Lasagna. Another one of our dinner party staples is lasagna. It's delicious and easy to make in large quantities. We loved the fact that we could make it in advance and it would taste just as good. We rejected this idea because our guests would be arriving at different times, and we didn't think cold lasagna sounded particularly appealing.

Ultimately, we decided that sandwiches would do the trick (and go along with the welcome picnic theme). They would be cheap and easy and could be served cold. Due to cost constraints, catering was out. We went with a friend's suggestion, a "create your own sandwich bar." I thought it was tacky at first but went back to my values and warmed to the idea. We also offered local chips and our favorite homemade dessert, brownie crumble and cherries with vanilla ice cream.

In the end, the meal at our welcome picnic was inconsequential. Our friends and family were just happy to see us, bask in the gloriousness of the Rocky Mountains, play football and volleyball, hang out in the hot tub, and meet each other.

For the reception, Matt and I had been tossing around the idea of a Mexican buffet because we both love Mexican food. Cathy and Cory, the innkeepers at Sunshine Mountain Inn, brainstormed with us. Cory's idea for a Mexican casserole planted the seed that maybe we could cater the thing ourselves. We started brainstorming other ideas: fajitas, tamales, make-your-own quesadillas, guacamole, salsa, seven-layer dip, chips. With only $500 allocated to our reception food, we had few options for actually getting the food. Even Cathy and Cory's generous offer to cater our reception for $15 a head wasn't going to work. At that point, we were anticipating about a hundred guests; $1,500 for catering would have been 75 percent of our budget.

We added a tab to the Excel sheet entitled "Food." We listed each item we were thinking about serving. In the next column we noted how far in advance it could be made. For anything that needed to be made the day before or the day of, we listed how long it would take to make it. Suddenly, self-catering our own reception for one hundred people seemed possible. We would buy and freeze tamales far in advance and make the fajitas, guacamole, salsa, and seven-layer dip the day before or the day of the event.

And then it occurred to me. What better way to spend quality time with our friends than to cook with them? Matt and I love cooking, and we love throwing dinner parties. We cook dinner together at least four times a week because it helps us stay connected to each other. The prospect of spending a few hours cooking with our friends on our wedding day actually seemed fun.

I did worry about overburdening our friends, however. I wanted them to be able to relax and enjoy the reception. With the extra money we would have left over from charging $25 to $35 for accommodations at Sunshine Mountain Lodge, we hired Cathy and Cory to heat up the food, set it out, refill it as necessary, and clean up, all for $50 an hour. That way, our friends could help with the preparation but then sit back and enjoy the fruits of their labor during the actual reception. Our last hurdle was to run the idea by a few other people. Although we wanted to retain complete control over our planning decisions to ensure that our wedding fully represented us as a couple, we didn't want our families to feel completely disenfranchised. We wanted them to look forward to the celebration and feel connected to the event.

I called my mom first. I tried to get through the self-catering part as fast as I could and get to the part where Cathy and Cory took care of everything during the reception. I called her first because she is generally supportive of my cockamamie ideas—at least outwardly supportive. She didn't balk or flip out. In fact, she sounded like she believed it was a generally doable idea, even if it wasn't the most brilliant one she had heard in a while. I even asked if she thought my stepdad might like to be in charge of cooking the fajitas. He's a great chef. If he had his druthers, he would probably own his own restaurant and cook all day. He was the best candidate for the position of fajita chef. He also has a huge heart and gives generously of himself and his time.

"Dan?" my mom called out. After pulling him away from the TV, she continued, "Sara wants to know if you'll cook fajitas at her wedding."

"No way." I could hear his emphatic answer through the phone and the thousand-plus miles that separated us. I think my mom and I were equally shocked by his refusal.

He elaborated: "I don't want to miss out on any of the fun. I don't want to be stuck cooking during the reception," he said frankly.

I explained that we could set up the grills in the main hangout area and he would be immersed in the fun. My mom relayed the message. No response.

I invented a line that would be useful throughout the wedding planning process when I needed to give someone a less awkward out: "Well, just take some time to think about it and let me know."

I said good-bye, hung up the phone, and started to cry.

Actions speak a heck of a lot louder than words. Although my family sounded supportive of our quest to keep our budget reasonable and plan a shindig that represented us, my stepdad's flat-out refusal to help make it happen was a slap in my emotional face. I was hurt.

I called my best friend, Andy, for the affirmation I needed, but he wasn't much help. He thought self-catering was a big mistake—too risky, difficult, time-consuming. He even supported his argument with a real-world example from a wedding he had recently attended. Even though the wedding was professionally catered, there still wasn't enough food. His argument went: "If a professional caterer can't estimate the quantities correctly, what makes you think you'll be able to?" He said he would make the salsa if I absolutely needed him to, but it was clear that he wouldn't be happy about it.

"No, don't worry about it," I said. "I'll find someone else."

I knew we had to have friends and family who would be excited to help. But if it wasn't my best friend or my stepfather, I wasn't sure who exactly it would be.

Eventually, I found the perfect fajita chef on our guest list and started finding friends who were eager to cook with us on our wedding day. My best friend wanted to join the cooking group. Our juicer broke, the fajita chef had a hard time juicing all the limes for the marinade, we started to run out of time, and we didn't have much time to get dressed for the ceremony, but despite all that, I have fond memories of cooking with my friends on my wedding day.

A big part of why self-catering worked for us was that we had built such strong relationships with the innkeepers at the B&B. Once we had the detailed wedding agenda figured out, we planned another visit to Sunshine Mountain Lodge. We liked Cathy and Cory and wanted to get to know them better. We also knew that the stronger our relationship was, the better our wedding experience would be. We volunteered to help in their garden, since they had mentioned that they would be planting extra flowers for our wedding.

When we arrived, they offered to take us out to lunch. They drove us to a local café with outdoor seating, nestled in the mountains. They asked us how our wedding planning was going, and we asked them about their own wedding. We also asked them about their lives in the mountains—how they made friends, what they did in their spare time.

When we started to talk through wedding logistics, our detailed agenda helped a lot. They were able to ask very specific questions, and we were able to clarify things (such as where to put the quesadilla maker and how many grills we could use).

Although we had originally been skeptical about Sunshine Mountain Lodge (it could fit only half our guests, the accommodations were rustic, there were stuffed moose everywhere), we quickly came to our senses. Cathy and Cory were the most wonderful people. They made wedding planning so much easier with their generosity and eagerness to help. They let us use all their tables for the reception, their grills, their Christmas lights, their coolers, their entire kitchen; the list goes on. They also volunteered to borrow more folding chairs from another B&B.

Once those logistics were settled, we turned our attention to our dessert and alcohol plans. We didn't want an expensive, traditional wedding cake, but we still wanted cake. We decided to buy several regular-size cakes. We searched around for a local bakery to meet our budgetary and dietary needs but couldn't seem to find one in Denver. That left us with one of our tried-and-true bakeries: Whole Foods.

On our next weekly trip to Whole Foods, we stopped by the bakery counter to assess the cake situation. We found an amazingly helpful (and generous-with-her-samples) baker who talked us through all the options. We opted for the following:

Carrot cake
Tiramisu
Apple tart
Turtle cheesecake
Chocolate Decadence
Berry Chantilly cake

On the low side, the woman estimated that our cakes would serve eighty people. On the high side: 110. She explained that we could place a special order, and they would make the cakes on the same day we needed them. We went ahead and paid for them in advance, since our friend was going to pick them up for us.

We paid $178 for six cakes, which was $22 under budget. Woo-hoo!

Although I am infatuated with the beauty of cake stands, I didn't spend any time stressing out about how to arrange and display the cakes. I figured most of our guests would be too focused on the cakes to care about the aesthetics of the serving table.

Unfortunately, coming up with our alcohol plan was more difficult. I quickly realized that planning a wedding is a little like trying to play both sides of a tennis court. On the one side, it's all about you. It's about sharing yourselves and your relationship with your nearest and dearest. On the other side of the court, it's about your guests. After all, you want them to have a good time. They are spending time and money to attend your wedding, and you want to honor their presence. Sometimes, these two sides are at odds, and trying to play both of them at the same time leaves you completely exhausted and in desperate need of a paramedic.

Take our alcohol situation. Our guests would have loved an open bar, but Matt and I didn't have the budget for it. We decided that the best way to come in under our designated $450 would be to serve only beer, wine, and a signature drink. Since we were serving Mexican-themed food at our wedding reception, we decided to serve frozen margaritas. A quick online search revealed that many places rent out frozen margarita machines. It would cost half our alcohol budget, but it was worth it for the fun factor.

As far as the wine goes, we pretty much had enough money for only boxed wine (much to the chagrin of pretty much everyone we know and love). When I told my aunt we were serving boxed wine at the reception, she replied (with vehemence), "Disgusting!"

Normally, that kind of response would not faze me. I know our country has a majorly bad taste in its mouth about boxed wine. But my aunt happens to be the most accepting, supportive, laid-back person I know. So her reaction was a huge shock. I had to keep telling myself: "It's about love, commitment, friendship, connection—not boxed wine."

Luckily, after more Internet scouring, we found a boxed wine taste test conducted by the *Austin Chronicle*. The paper had slipped bottled wine (in the $15 to $20 range) into the blind taste test. For the most part, the judges picked the bottled wine. But there were three exceptions. And those were the three boxed wines we decided to purchase for our wedding reception:

Seeberger Riesling ($16 for three liters)
Powers Columbia Valley 2003 Cabernet Sauvignon ($20 for three liters)
Hardys Stamp Merlot ($16 for three liters)

After we decided to purchase boxed wine, we read an op-ed piece in the *New York Times* about the environmental benefits of boxed wine. Apparently, bottled wine has a much greater carbon footprint because it's that much heavier to ship. I didn't even realize we were being more eco-friendly by going the boxed wine route.

We had an equally hard time trying to figure out what to do about beer. I sent a survey to a few of my beer-drinking guests to gather their opinions.

Voter A wrote, "Can't go wrong with any of the domestics (Bud, Michelob . . .) My vote would be Budweiser and Coors Light (brewed in Colorado) . . . and, they cost less than the imports!"

The very next e-mail I received was from Voter B: "Here's what I'd suggest, if beer snobbery is as rampant among your loved ones as mine: strike a balance between quality and affordability, and avoid Coors products at all costs."

Oy vey. We decided to put off making the decision for a while.

We let our friend Mike (also known as our alcohol manager) decide on our final beer choices. We went with Miller Light in a big keg and New Belgium Sunshine Wheat in a small keg. The Sunshine Wheat went quickly. People didn't seem to mind the Miller Light (although they may have complained about it behind our backs). The novelty and freedom of an open-access keg at a wedding seemed to keep the drinkers very happy.

When it came to reception decorations, Matt and I budgeted precisely $50. We weren't sure what we meant by decorations, but we figured we might want to have some. This number also included any flowers we decided to purchase (yes, even for my wedding bouquet). We kept the number intentionally low (only 2.5 percent of our budget) because we valued everything else so much more.

The first thing we decided to spend our decoration money on was tablecloths. Cathy and Cory had agreed to let us use their folding tables. Many of the tables were in good condition, but they were plastic and unmatched. We thought about purchasing cheap cloth and fashioning it into tablecloths. In the end, however, we decided go with used sheets instead. It was the perfect way to be eco- and budget-friendly (although it was a little gross). We took to scouring resale shops in search of used but not disgusting sheets. We managed to find perfectly acceptable sheets (referred to as tablecloths from here on out).

And when the wedding porn started making me doubt all my choices and making me feel deeply insecure (again), I repeated my mantra: "A wedding is about commitment, community, connection, and fun—not aesthetically pleasing table settings."

We toyed with the idea of using potted flowers from our garden as centerpieces, but our thumbs weren't exactly green in Colorado. In the end, we decided that the appetizers would be enough of a centerpiece.

Also, we had decided against assigned seating, so we didn't need to worry about table numbers or name cards. It made sense for a couple of reasons. First, we were serving the food buffet-style. Secondly, we wanted to create the more casual feeling of a family reunion.

And then there was the issue of plates, cups, and forks.

We wanted to use real tableware because it is much better for the environment than anything disposable (plus it looks better). But we couldn't figure out how to make it work. In the end we decided to go with disposable stuff. To stay aligned with our eco-friendly values, we found compostable bowls, cups, forks, and spoons on the Internet. We found compostable plates at Sam's Club.

The other component of the reception that we needed to figure out was the professional photography. Matt and I decided not to have professional photographers for several reasons:

- It wasn't in our budget. We didn't want to go into debt, and we wanted to save money for our first house.
- We have three great friends who are perfectly good photographers.
- Matt and I had never hired a professional photographer for any other major event, and our wedding didn't feel any different to us.

We entrusted the duty to three people because we didn't want any one person to feel responsible for capturing the entire wedding and because we hadn't seen any of their work in a long time, so we didn't want to put all our eggs in one basket. Then we came up with very specific directions about what we were looking for and what kind of photos we wanted.

In addition to planning the specific photos, we also created a very specific agenda (with times, to-do items, and directions) so we could share our vision with Cathy and Cory, as well as all the friends and family who were coordinating different aspects of our wedding. Our approach required a lot of upfront planning, but the smooth execution made it all worth it.

BUILDING RELATIONSHIPS WITH VENDORS

Unless your entire wedding is orchestrated by friends and family (which is possible), you'll be hiring vendors. The quicker you build solid relationships with your vendors, the smoother your wedding planning process will be. The goal is to trust your vendors 100 percent and for the vendors to be eager to help you because they like you.

Although each vendor situation is unique, there are some consistent ways to build relationships:

- Hire only vendors you like. Yes, this point seems entirely obvious, but you might be tempted to hire the cheapest vendor to stay within your budget. In some cases that may make sense (such as chair delivery), but in other cases it makes sense to prioritize relationships above price. For example, you wouldn't want a photographer you didn't like to follow you around all day.
- Ask everyone you know for leads; you might be surprised who's connected to whom. Also, once you find and trust a vendor, ask that

person for additional recommendations. If you can't find a vendor you like and trust, consider whether family or friends could handle the task or whether it's something you can do without.

- Ask vendors about themselves and their lives. Most people want to feel heard, so ask and then listen.
- Sincerely compliment your vendors for the work they do. Often, we say nice things about people behind their backs rather than to their faces. Share with them how much you enjoy and appreciate what they have to offer. Caution: Don't be fake! This strategy works only if you are authentic.
- Follow up with a thank-you card or e-mail during the wedding planning process, not just at the end. Taking a few minutes to put your thoughts and feelings into a note can mean a lot to someone. The investment of time usually pays off in huge dividends.
- After the wedding, if you were happy with certain vendors, recommend them to others and offer to serve as a reference for them. Help another couple have the same positive experience you did.

CATERING

You want to provide your guests with the most delicious food possible (whether it's a three-course meal or simply wine and cheese), but you don't want the catering bill to eat up your entire budget. Here are a few ideas for saving money:

- Avoid major meal times. This is the standard recommendation for brides on a budget. There are a couple of variations on this theme, including having a brunch wedding or serving champagne and cake instead of a full-blown meal. Or maybe throw an ice-cream sundae party, or a reception catered by an ice-cream truck!
- Host a potluck and let your community cater the meal. Potlucks are taboo in the wedding world, but I've never understood why. To me, asking your friends and family to contribute a small piece of themselves is an amazing way to build community and connection. Further, it's the way weddings were done for hundreds of years before consumerism took over. It's also fun and adventurous!
- Self-cater. Matt and I went this route because we wanted to save money and involve our community in the creation of our wedding. Although this route worked nearly perfectly for us, it's not something to be undertaken lightly. It takes a lot of planning and can create a ton of stress.

- Partially self-cater. If a handful of your nearest and dearest like to cook, why not tap into their culinary skills for all the side dishes and hire a catering company to provide the main dishes, or vice versa?
- Go for novelty. Rent a portable wood-burning oven plus a pizza crew, or hire an entire taco truck. You might have cheaper options, but these will certainly go a long way toward making the day memorable.
- Stray far from the beaten path. There are deals waiting to be scored in the dives and family-run businesses of our towns. Think of your favorite restaurant (that doesn't have a preprinted catering menu) and talk to them about the possibilities. What about finding an up-and-coming caterer who is looking to build his or her portfolio? Or what about friends of friends of friends? You can use Craigslist to hire additional serving, cleaning, and setting up help—or hire younger siblings' friends.

Remember, expensive does not necessarily equal good. I have been to plenty of expensive weddings at expensive venues that essentially served conference- or airplane-quality food. The moral of the story is: Be creative, work within your vision, and consider stepping outside of the wedding formula. Your wedding is your chance to share your lives with your nearest and dearest, and every choice about how that happens is yours.

DESSERT

What kind of dessert do you like to eat? Serve it! If you want a traditional cake at your wedding but can't afford the expense, look into culinary schools or friends of friends who might be able to create the same product for a fraction of the normal cost. Alternatively, consider getting a small fancy cake and keeping a big inexpensive sheet cake in the back. If you like cake but could take or leave wedding cake in particular, serve several different smaller cakes.

If you prefer pies or cookies, set up a table of various options that you purchase, make yourself, or ask close friends and family to bring. Many desserts can be made in advance and frozen, so self-catering the dessert options is absolutely doable.

DISTURBING ADVICE FROM THE WEDDING INDUSTRIAL COMPLEX

"After the wedding dress, the bride probably spends more time and thought on the wedding cake than anything else. This is the centerpiece of the reception, the item everyone gets to sample and it has to be perfect from the inside out. From the bottom to the top."

—www.transworldnews.com, November, 13, 2008

Prefer to go the quirky route? Set up an ice-cream sundae bar or hire an ice-cream truck. Or set up plain cupcakes or cookies and let guests frost and decorate them. What about serving favorite desserts from your childhoods with recipes provided by friends and family?

The point is, dessert is yet another area of wedding planning that can be full of "shoulds" and "musts." But it doesn't have to be that way. Think about what you want and make it happen!

ALCOHOL PLAN

When it comes to planning the alcohol for your wedding, there are lots of factors to consider:

- What kind of alcohol do we want (if any)?
- What kind of alcohol would our guests prefer?
- What can we afford?

Essentially, your alcohol plan is at the intersection of these three circles. Of course, I'm making the decision sound much easier than it is, but you have to find the decision that feels right to you.

When Allison planned a wedding in Cape Cod, she started "stalking [the] local board on TheKnot.com for months and was feeling guilty about not having an open bar." She continued, "Then I remembered that the past four weddings I attended locally had cash bars, and at the time I thought nothing of it." Ultimately, she and her partner decided to go with a cash bar.

Marina and Zack decided not to serve any alcohol at their wedding. Their wedding website FAQ page read: "Will there be alcohol at the reception? Nope! Both Zack and Marina have more fun without it, and are planning all sorts of good shindigs so you will too." Marina explained, "We had a few people who were a little unhappy about it, but since the reception ended fairly early (9 p.m.), most of the people who wanted alcohol went and had alcohol afterward. The best way to respond to questions was to remind people that Zack and I weren't planning on drinking, and watching everyone else get drunk was not our idea of a good time. Not much you can say to that."

Callie and Dave decided on a hybrid approach. They got "a bottle of wine for each table then an open bar just past dinner and cash until the end of the night."

Look at your budget, generate a list of various options, imagine each option in your mind to see how it would play out, check it against your vision of your wedding, and then make a decision. Once you've made your decision, don't torture yourself by wondering if you've made the right one. It's definitely not going to make or break your wedding!

SIGNATURE DRINKS

Offering a signature drink can be a great way to bridge the divide between an open bar and beer and wine only. Because they can be made in bulk, signature drinks cost significantly less than an open bar, yet they still provide hard liquor for people who are looking for something stronger than beer and wine. Some fun options include:

Sangria
Martinis (apple, chocolate, blueberry)
Gimlets
Cosmopolitans
Bay Breezes
Mojitos
Daiquiris
Mint juleps
Jell-O shots anyone?

TABLEWARE, CENTERPIECES, AND VENUE DECORATIONS

The September 2008 issue of *Brides* magazine said, "Guests gaze at them all night, so each little accent—place cards, menus, and votives, should be a tiny treasure." With pressure like that, it's easy to start spending significant energy on things that have a negligible impact on the quality of your guests' experience (and your own, for that matter).

There's nothing wrong with putting some time, energy, and money into tableware, centerpieces, and venue decorations, but don't lose sight of more important things, such as building community, fostering connection, and having fun.

Avoid stress and unnecessary cost (both fiscally and environmentally) by coming up with a plan that:

- Fits in your budget. Be honest with yourself about how much money it makes sense to spend on tableware, centerpieces, and decorations. Apply the 10-10-10 Rule if necessary. Ask yourself how important these items will seem in ten minutes, ten months, and ten years.
- Satisfies your aesthetic—enough. Remember: No one is going to be looking at the decorations the way you will be looking at them when you're setting them up. The decorations are merely going to be part of a larger context. Instead of staring at the centerpieces, your guests will be staring into the faces of old friends. Instead of analyzing the napkins, guests will be craning their necks to see the look on your dad's face during the toasts. (Be sure not to block their view with oversized centerpieces!)

- Feels respectful of the environment. Buying something in bulk and using it once takes a huge toll on the environment. You can reduce waste (and get great deals) by shopping on websites that connect couples who want to buy and sell wedding paraphernalia. Also, think about reusing things at your own wedding, such as using ceremony decorations at the reception or using wedding favors as centerpieces. Compostable dishware is available. You could also scour thrift stores for secondhand plates and cups or buy used catering dishware (search for "dish sets" on Craigslist). After the wedding, these items can be resold, donated, or used for other big parties.

- Keeps you grounded. Sure, a thousand origami cranes (a symbol of peace) might fit in your budget and satisfy your aesthetic, but will you stress yourself out (and send yourself to the doctor's office with a serious case of carpal tunnel syndrome) in the process of making them? Maybe or maybe not. Maybe you'll have friends over for a fondue and folding party. Just don't stress yourself out over something that ultimately doesn't matter all that much.

Allison helps keep it in perspective. At first she was focused "on all the fine details and was ready to dish out an extra forty cents for blue versus white napkins." Then she "thought back to the weddings [she] had been to" and realized that she "could only remember three big things from each wedding: 1. Food; 2. Music; 3. The thank-you note."

PHOTOGRAPHY AND VIDEOGRAPHY

Photography and videography can easily commandeer a large share of your wedding budget. To cut down on costs, consider these options:

- Ask a friend. Looking over your guest list might reveal a friend with a fancy camera who might enjoy experiencing the event through his or her lens. Or perhaps a friend of a friend might give you a serious discount on photography.

- Find someone who is building his or her portfolio. Lots of people with day jobs, as well as students in photography and videography programs, want to build their professional experience. They can offer high-quality photography on a shoestring budget. Ask everyone you know for a connection or look on sites like Craigslist.

- Keep it in perspective. As you're comparing options and deciding on packages, identify any pressure you're feeling from friends, family, or the wedding industrial complex about what you're *supposed to do* when it comes to wedding photography and videography. I've heard people say, "The photos are the only tangible thing you're going to have after the wedding" (um, what about your *lifetime partner*?) or "The photos are reason enough to have a wedding." As with every wedding decision, think about what will matter in ten minutes, ten months, and ten years and go from there.

Some questions to help guide photography planning:

- What formal photos do you want to be sure your photographer captures? Make a list and get input from key people to make sure they get the photos they want as well (within reason, of course).
- Do you want some fun shots during the formal photography session? A photographer could easily have everyone smile for the first shot and jump for the second shot.
- Do you want your photographer to keep snapping during transitions to capture more candid shots (such as hugs or special looks)?
- What else do you want your photographer to be sure to capture? Friends and family setting up for the reception? Children on the dance floor?

Consider appointing someone to be in charge of corralling groups together for formal shots. Also, be strategic about the order of the shots, so that people can join the party as soon as their pictures are taken. For example, take photos of large groups first so that more people can return to the party early.

As with any vendor, be sure you communicate with your photographer clearly and specifically ahead of time about your wants, needs, and expectations. You want to be on the same page to avoid any disappointment. Consider also whether you or trusted family or friends should check in with the photographer during the day to make any minor course corrections.

PHOTOS FROM GUESTS

We chose not to go with a professional photographer, but we still ended up with more than two thousand photos. Abracadabra!

Honestly, it was easy. We set up an account through www.flickr.com. Although we already had an account on that website, we created a new one, so we would be more comfortable sharing the user name and password with our guests.

We upgraded the account for a small yearly fee so we would have unlimited storage. On our wedding website, we told guests ahead of time that we'd want them to upload their photos afterward. After the wedding, we sent out a reminder e-mail with the user name and password. The experiment worked beautifully! We ended up with plenty of pictures—all from different perspectives.

A couple other ways to capture your guests' photos:

- Set up a downloading station. At the reception, set up a laptop and a card reader for folks to use. Either ask someone to supervise the station or provide detailed instructions.
- Send out blank CDs with return envelopes. I'm not a big fan of this option because of the waste it creates (both environmentally and fiscally), but it works for some people.

MUSIC

Here are three questions that can help drive your decision about music at your wedding:

- What kind of music do we want at our wedding (if any)?
- What kind of music would our guests prefer to hear?
- What can we afford?

Your answers might lead you to a live band, a deejay, providing your own music (via something like an iPod), or having no music at all. Each of these options has its own benefits and drawbacks. For example, live bands provide energy, but they also need to take breaks, which can interject lulls into the evening. Deejays are good at reading the crowd and matching the music accordingly, but they can also be expensive and annoying. Providing your own music is a cost-effective solution, but it takes effort to generate an appropriate playlist.

As with all wedding-related decisions, think through the benefits and drawbacks of each option and make a decision that feels right to you. Realize if you're working within a limited budget, you won't be able to have it all. Remember to tap into your network of family and friends: Maybe you know someone in a band who can lend you high-quality speakers. Maybe a friend of a friend is a deejay and can give you a discount. Think creatively. Ask yourself what options you might have unconsciously ruled out and revisit them.

HOW TO DEEJAY YOUR OWN WEDDING

FIND A WAY TO PROJECT THE SOUND PROFESSIONALLY

I love dancing and wanted our wedding reception to evolve into a thumping, jumping, full-blown p-a-r-t-y. However, I worried that with anything less than professional sound equipment, we would have trouble corralling enough energy and interest for true get-down dancing. We researched options for renting equipment (via rental companies and a Craigslist posting; amateur musicians also often have nice equipment). In the process, we realized we had a friend in a band. Matt contacted him, and Nick agreed to let us borrow his stuff for the night. He also volunteered to be in charge of transporting it, setting it up, and breaking it down.

CREATE SEPARATE PLAYLISTS

Once the equipment situation was settled, Matt got to work creating playlists. He created a preceremony playlist, a postceremony playlist, a dinner playlist, and a dance party playlist. There's no right or wrong answer to the question of what to play. We started with music we liked and thought about which specific songs would create the kind of ambience we were going for.

MATCH THE ARC OF THE MUSIC TO THE ARC OF THE EVENT

Deejays are skilled at matching music to the mood and using music to further shape the mood. If you don't have a deejay, you have to take matters into your own hands. Anticipate the arc of the event and create playlists that align with that arc. For example, we started our dinner mix with relaxing yet upbeat music. When the dancing started, we switched it up. We started with a few classic, popular dance tunes to get people out on the floor early. We folded slow songs into the mix to give people time to rest. Don't worry too much about planning everything in perfect detail—you can always advance to different songs throughout the event, if needed, to match the energy of the crowd.

GET SUGGESTIONS FROM GUESTS

I love the trend of asking friends and family to request songs on their RSVPs. It's a fun way to build community and connection.

BRING A BACKUP DEVICE

It's less stressful to plan ahead for a problem than to scramble at the last minute. We brought a backup iPod in case something went wrong. Don't forget your power and charging devices either.

PLAN ANY INTRODUCTIONS

We wanted someone to introduce our first dance, so we asked Nick to do the honors. You can also create custom introductions (such as "This song goes out to Grandma") by recording them in the correct format and inserting them in the playlist.

CLEARLY ESTABLISH ROLES AND RESPONSIBILITIES IN ADVANCE

Think about what equipment needs to be where and when, and how it will get there. For example, who will bring the speakers? What time will he or she bring them? Where exactly will the speakers be set up? How many outlets will be needed? Will any additional cords be needed? Who is bringing the iPod and the backup? What time should the music start? Who will press the "play" button? Answering these questions (and any others) will help make the event run smoothly.

DECIDE YOUR POLICY ON GUESTS HANDLING YOUR EQUIPMENT

Matt and I didn't figure out a policy before the wedding, and one friend didn't like our choice in music and kept trying to change it. In retrospect, I wish we had secured the iPod beneath a sheet of paper (with the edges taped down), with a note that said, "Please respect our music choices." It could be fun to have guests involved with the music, but that didn't work for us.

LET GO AND IMMERSE YOURSELF IN THE MOMENT

You don't want your wedding to fly by, and you don't want to be a bundle of nerves. Once you've planned everything that is in your control, surrender to the universe and truly experience the sheer loveliness of bringing together your family and friends to witness and celebrate your commitment. Even if there is a major snafu with the music, trust that someone will figure out a solution. Case in point: The power went out at my friend's wedding, and some of her former students banded together and started singing. It was very moving and memorable.

Overall, we were pleased with our DIY iPod wedding reception. The dance party was a blast. The money we saved (and diverted toward a down payment two days after our wedding weekend) was definitely worth it. Plus, we had a great experience working with our friend Nick, and he seemed more connected to the experience because he played an integral role in it.

WEDDING FAVORS

To ensure "the perfect day," many people want all the little details to be just right: favors for the guests, out-of-towner bags, gifts for the wedding party. But once again, the magic word is *choice*. You can pick and choose what you want for your own wedding. You can reject everything wholeheartedly and vehemently if you want. You can add new things and create your own traditions.

Matt and I decided to make wedding favors because we liked the idea of giving our guests a small token of appreciation for making the trip all the way to Colorado. We wanted to make the favors as meaningful as possible, as well as reflective of our values (and they had to be cheap, cheap, cheap). We decided to make cilantro seed packets with our famous cilantro guacamole recipe and directions for planting the seeds. We wanted to encourage our friends and family to cook and to sow seeds, which are two of our favorite things. The favors looked beautiful (except that I placed the guacamole recipe too low on the back of the packet and ended up sewing right through it). However, I'm not sure they were worth the time and effort, and somehow we wound up with leftovers despite making only one per guest.

Virginia and Dan "didn't want to give people something they would just take home and throw away," so they decided to "turn the favors into a wedding event." Virginia's mom is British, and her family always opens "crackers" (paper tubes that have hidden surprises inside) at Christmas. She decided to make crackers for the wedding. She and Dan "got the entire 120-person crowd to [open them] together right before dinner. Inside was a brightly colored tissue paper crown, which everyone wore while eating and dancing, and a cartoon of Dan and myself, thanking everyone for coming and telling them that we had made a donation on their behalf to the Central Asia Institute, a charity we both support."

Amanda and Ryan, who married in 2009, "just said NO" to wedding favors. Amanda explained, "I can't remember ever savoring or even remembering wedding favors."

If you want to buy or create favors, think through the cost in terms of money, time, effort, and stress and decide if satisfying your generous impulse is worth what it takes. You might love making favors and feel good about the personal touch. You might find a local artisan or vendor to make favors (chocolates, for example). Or you might skip favors entirely. They're a nice touch, but keep your perspective, make your decision, and move on.

ENTERTAINING KIDS

What about children at your wedding? This can be a touchy subject. Some approaches include:

- Ask guests to leave their kids at home—politely, of course, with a carefully worded note on the invitation or your wedding website. (Be sure to provide special assistance to out-of-town guests who might need a babysitter or equipment such as a car seat or crib.)
- Ask parents to bring their own entertainment for their children or to immerse their children in the wedding fun, such as by shaking it down as a family on the dance floor.
- Provide age-appropriate entertainment such as coloring books, modeling clay, hopscotch, lawn games, board games, a movie and popcorn area, or a bouncy house—depending on the ages of your guests' children.

- Offer child care by hiring teenagers or friends of friends to supervise a kid's area. Or organize a little babysitting co-op where each parent spends thirty minutes watching all the children in exchange for having the rest of the evening child-free.

The decision will depend on your unique circumstances. How many of your guests have children and would want to bring them? What are their ages? How hurt or angry would the parents be about being asked not to bring the children? Would the request affect your relationship in the future? Are you close to the children and do you want them at your wedding? Will the event be appropriate for children? What's your budget?

Once you've made a decision that feels right to you, communicate it kindly and clearly with your guests well ahead of the event, so that everyone understands the plan. Think about how to handle any last-minute issues, such as babysitter problems causing guests to bring children you hadn't planned on.

IDEAS FOR NEXT STEPS

- Brainstorm ideas for how to build relationships with your vendors. The stronger your relationships, the more smoothly your wedding is likely to unfold.
- Brainstorm and explore all your catering options, including for dessert. Don't forget to venture off the beaten path.
- Think through your preferences for alcohol. What makes the most sense for you as a couple (and for your budget)? Do you want an open bar for the entire night or part of the night? Do you want just beer and wine? Just champagne? No alcohol at all?
- Make a plan for tableware, centerpieces, and venue decorations. Remember that these things are the more inconsequential aspects of your event. Your guests are going to be caught up in the emotion of the wedding. They won't be staring at the table settings. I swear.
- Explore your options for photography and videography. Decide which (if any) formal photos you want taken.
- Create a system to get photos from your guests.
- Figure out your approach to music at the reception, wedding favors, and entertaining kids.
- Have fun and remember that the details don't matter as much as the substance of your wedding!

Melissa + Alex
Guacamole Recipe
Ingredients
❑ 4 ripe avocados ❑ 1/3 cup diced red onion ❑ ½ tbs. diced jalapeno pepper ❑ 1/3 cup diced tomato ❑ 1/6 cup fresh cilantro chopped ❑ 1 tbs. lemon juice ❑ ¾ tsp. sea salt
Directions
1. Scrape the inside of the avocados into a bowl.
2. Mash the avocados with a fork to about 75% of your preferred end consistency, since there's still more mashing to come.
3. Add the onion, jalapeño, cilantro, lemon juice, and sea salt. Stir.
4. Add the tomatoes and stir slightly.
5. Serve! (with chips that aren't too flimsy).
love

DIY Project 9:

WEDDING FAVOR SEED PACKETS

These DIY wedding favor seed packets are budget-friendly and Earth-friendly, but they do take some time to make. Choose a recipe you're known for, a family recipe, or one that links to your venue or city somehow and choose seeds that relate to the recipe. Make sure to include directions for planting the seeds and caring for the plants.

MATERIALS

Cardstock (each piece of 8 ½x11" stock makes two seed packets)
Thread
A sewing machine
Seeds in bulk
A paper cutter, scissors, or craft knife
A stamp (sized to fit your packet)
An ink pad

Tip: Consider making your own stamp using the tutorial on page 101.

DIRECTIONS

1. Use a word processing or design program to lay out the planting instructions on the front and the recipe on the back. You can download the template we used at http://2000dollarwedding.com.
2. Print the planting instructions on one side of each card. Feed the cardstock through the printer again to print the recipe on the other side.
3. Use a paper cutter, scissors, or craft knife to chop the cardstock in half.
4. Use a stamp to print an image on the bottom half of the card. (Make sure it's upside down, since you will fold the card to create a pouch for the seeds.) Alternatively, you could insert clip art during the design stage.
5. Sew around the three outside edges to create a pouch.
6. Fill the pouch with seeds.
7. Sew across the top to close the pouch.

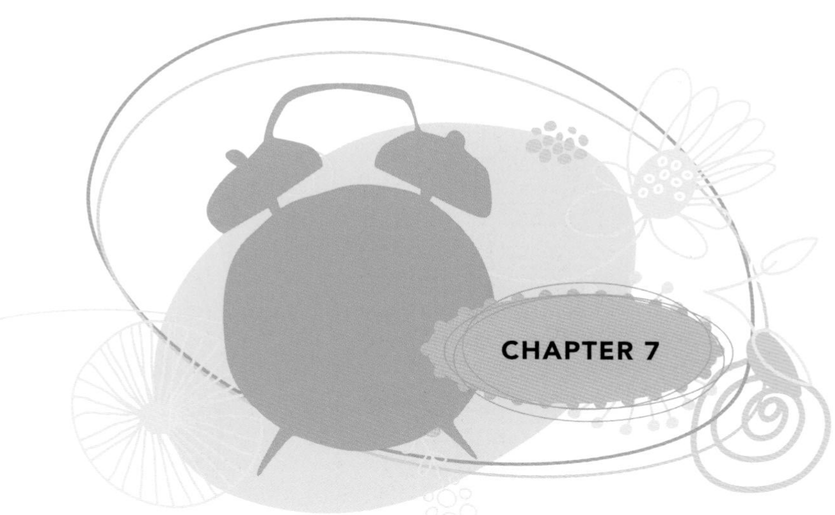

THE COUNTDOWN: Getting It All Done and Staying Sane

You're getting so close! To ensure that you're as prepared and organized as possible for your wedding day, this chapter talks about creating a detailed wedding agenda (and includes an example), a list of everything you need to bring to the wedding, and detailed job descriptions. Then we delve deeper into the emotional aspects of this part of planning, including making sure your wedding doesn't overshadow your relationship, coping with family conflict, and experiencing a range of emotions.

I give advice for taking shortcuts on things that don't really matter and crossing off nonessential items. This section starts with Matt's and my story about how we got everything done and stayed sane. It ends with specific ideas for next steps.

OUR STORY

I get a little stressed just thinking about the days leading up to our wedding. Not only did we have to shop for all the food for two communal meals and pack everything for the wedding, we also had to pack our entire house.

On the day before we left for the wedding venue, we went shopping for all the food items we needed for the welcome picnic and wedding reception. We started at Sam's Club and had carts full of food. We hadn't thought to specify quantities of items when we made our lists, so we had to make real-time decisions about how much of everything to buy. What a tedious process. I resorted to calling different people to ask for their input: "How many limes do you think we need for the fajita marinade?"

Matt and I got into a fight in the produce aisle because the store had only rock-hard avocados, and Matt wanted to purchase them. "But they won't be ready in time!" I insisted, cringing at the thought of trying to make guacamole with anything but ripe avocados. "We'll just put them in paper bags. They'll be ready by Friday," Matt assured me.

We called Matt's mom for advice. After some Internet searching, she agreed that they would be ready by Friday. Before we purchased the sixty-four avocados, I made Matt promise that we could go over budget and buy ripe avocados at the last minute if the first batch wasn't ready in time.

After filling two carts top to bottom with food at Sam's Club, we scrambled over to King Soopers to purchase a few more items. We ended the day at Whole Foods, where I found my vegetarian self standing helplessly at the meat counter trying to order pounds and pounds of fajita meat (with more phone calls to friends) and at the deli counter ordering more and more pounds of turkey, ham, and roast beef. Through the blur, it was impossible to tell if we were staying within our budget. I tried doing the math in my head, but the quantities were making it difficult.

In addition to purchasing all the food, I needed to hem the sheets into tablecloths. I was dreading this task because I have trouble sewing large things in straight lines. When I finally got around to washing the sheets in preparation for sewing, I realized that mice had chewed big holes in some of them. The situation could have played out in one of two ways:

- I burst into tears and exclaim (in elevated and piercing tones) that my day is ruined. My fiancé rushes to my side in an attempt to soothe me. He says, "We'll solve this problem by buying real tablecloths. Brand-new ones!"
- I say to myself, "Our wedding is about community, commitment, connection, and fun—not tablecloths."

Luckily, I picked door number two. I never did get around to hemming the tablecloths that didn't have big holes in them. I just handed them over to the owners of the B&B and let them work their magic. They ended up folding the extra fabric underneath the tablecloths—a simple, low-effort solution. Brilliant!

THE DETAILED WEDDING AGENDA

Since hiring a wedding coordinator would probably have cost our entire budget, we had to coordinate the details ourselves. Luckily, I love planning. However, even though we assumed the role of wedding coordinators leading up to our wedding, we didn't want to play the role *during* our wedding. We just wanted to sit back and enjoy the ride on our wedding day.

The key to making that possible was putting in a lot of planning up front, and one important aspect of the planning process was creating a detailed wedding agenda. I didn't want to micromanage myself to the minute, but I did want to have a clear picture of what to do and when. The agenda also helped clarify what we needed to communicate to other people.

The wedding agenda is a play-by-play of what's going to happen and how it's going to get done. Putting together the wedding agenda can help you and your partner identify decisions that still need to be made and details that still need to be sorted out. Centralizing all events and tasks in one document can help reduce anxiety and ensure that everything gets taken care of. (Although, even if it doesn't, you'll still be married in the end, and you might have a great story to tell.) Some things to include in your detailed wedding agenda:

- Times
- Locations
- Specific action items
- Person responsible for each action
- Materials needed

FINALIZING THE TO-BRING LIST

To be effective wedding planners for ourselves, it wasn't enough to have a detailed wedding agenda; we also had to create a to-bring list. Throughout the wedding planning process, we kept an ongoing list of everything we needed to bring to the wedding. In Excel, we had one column for the category (reception, welcome picnic, ceremony, getting ready, and so on), another column for the item to bring, and a third column for the name of the person who was supposed to bring it.

When we were purchasing rings, I added rings and the ring hat to the list. When Beth and I figured out a plan for my hair, I added hair products and bobby pins to the list. Because we were doing so much of the wedding

Our Detailed Wedding Agenda

Our play-by-play wedding agenda started on Tuesday with our shopping expedition and ended with our departure the day after the wedding. Here's an excerpt of the agenda from the ceremony and reception day:

Time		Event	Doer	Notes
Morning	☐	Peter washes the cloth napkins and hot tub towels.	Peter	
8–10	☐	Guests of Sunshine Mountain eat breakfast.	Guests	
10–11:45	☐	Wedding party goes to Meeker to set up and rehearse.	Wedding party	
12–12:45	☐	Wedding party goes to family lunch.	Wedding party	
1–3	☐	Cooking crew prepares guacamole, salsa, seven-layer dip, corn/bean salad, quesadilla fixin's, and fajitas.	Wedding party	
2:30	☐	Christy arrives with cakes and needs help unloading them.	Cathy & Cory	
2:30	☐	Christy arrives with the margarita machine and needs help unloading it.	Mike & Tom	
2–2:45	☐	Matt and Sara hike at Sunshine.	Matt & Sara	
2:45	☐	Sara takes shower.	Sara	
3:00	☐	Beth does Sara's hair.	Beth	
3:30	☐	Andy arrives at Meeker to oversee arrival of guests.	Andy	
4:00	☐	Guests start arriving at Meeker.	Guests	
4:00	☐	Matt and Sara leave Sunshine.	Matt & Sara	
by 4:30	☐	Cathy and Cory set up three grills on ground in front of deck.	Cathy & Cory	
by 4:30	☐	Cathy and Cory set up tables and chairs for eating on deck.	Cathy & Cory	
by 4:30	☐	Cathy and Cory set up serving tables on ground in front of deck.	Cathy & Cory	

Time		Event	Doer	Notes
	☐	Cathy and Cory set up quesadilla station and fixin's.	Cathy & Cory	
	☐	Cathy and Cory set up Crock-Pot with nacho cheese.	Cathy & Cory	
before ceremony	☐	Mike and Tom set up bar area inside the kitchen.	Mike & Tom	
	☐	Cathy and Cory set up paper products and napkins on serving table.	Cathy & Cory	
	☐	Cathy and Cory set up drinks, cups, and ice in kitchen area.	Cathy & Cory	
	☐	Cathy and Cory set out chips, guacamole, seven-layer dip, and salsa on tables in grove and on deck.	Cathy & Cory	
before ceremony	☐	Nick sets up sound system for dancing.	Nick	
by 4:30	☐	Cathy and Cory set up tables on volleyball court (with tablecloths and potted flowers).	Cathy & Cory	
5:30	☐	Guests start arriving at Sunshine.	Guests	
5:30	☐	Cathy and Cory steam tamales and set them out on serving tables.	Cathy & Cory	
5:30	☐	Brent cooks the fajitas.	Brent	
5:30	☐	Cathy and Cory set up the shredded cheese and sour cream for the fajitas (we will also use the guacamole and salsa from the chips).	Cathy & Cory	
	☐	Cathy and Cory refill chips, guacamole, salsa, cheese, tamales, ice, and sour cream.	Cathy & Cory	
7:30	☐	Cathy and Cory move tables off the patio for dancing.	Cathy & Cory	The tables can just be arranged on the flat dirt on the east side of the patio.
7:45	☐	Cathy and Cory start clearing off deck and moving leftovers to the kitchen counter.	Cathy & Cory	
8:15	☐	Cathy and Cory move the cakes to the tables on the ground in front of the deck.	Cathy & Cory	Table should be pushed against railing so guests can stand below and have a view.
	☐	Matt and Sara give thank-you speech to guests and helpers while Cathy and Cory start cutting the cake.	Cathy & Cory	
8:45	☐	Wedding party performs dance on flagstone patio.	Wedding party	Nick will start the song.

ourselves, the list grew massive. However, when it was time to pack the car and leave, we were able to just run through the list and make sure we packed everything.

I know lots of list makers who sprinkle their lists throughout the house: on sticky notes, napkins, the backs of envelopes. Although I definitely have the same tendencies, I have forced myself to centralize my lists. For the wedding, I kept all my lists in an Excel document (of course it doesn't have to be Excel). Being a disciplined list maker kept me sane while planning a massive event.

CREATING JOB DESCRIPTIONS

If your wedding is going to be a "barn raising" in the sense that you are going to bring together a large number of people and essentially say, "Please help us do what we can't do by ourselves," then you'll want to provide everyone with meticulous instructions about what—exactly—you want them to do; what role they're fulfilling; what tasks they're doing. If you don't, then you'll either have to act like an overseer at your own wedding, supervising and directing everybody as they undertake their tasks and fielding lots of questions, or give up all control of the outcomes.

Setting expectations and answering questions in the weeks leading up to the wedding can ensure that you can be fully present and immersed in the wedding when it happens. This advance work will also give you a sense of where you might run into problems, need additional help for those performing tasks, or have other difficulties. You might decide to let go of the reins and go with the flow of the best intentions and efforts of your family and friends, removing the focus on the outcome and appreciating their contributions.

For many tasks, it can be helpful to type up specific instructions about the where, when, and how. Yes, that's a lot of work up front, but it's worth it in the end, because you won't have to answer those questions during the actual experience. You want people to be completely empowered to take their jobs and run with them.

For example, here are the directions I typed up for Nick, the sound manager:

JOB:
Sound Manager

Things to Know:
Thank you, thank you, thank you for your contribution to the wedding. Seriously, we couldn't pull it off without your help.

You don't need to worry about any sound on Friday night. Matt will set up our little speaker.

You can decide whether to set up the sound before or after the ceremony on Saturday. The reception is at Sunshine Mountain Lodge, and the ceremony is six miles north on Hwy. 7 at Meeker Park Lodge. The ceremony at Meeker starts at 4:30 and will probably go until 5ish.

The sound should be set up on the flagstone patio at the back of the main house. The sliding glass doors lead out to the patio, and there is a half-wall along the edge of the patio. We were envisioning the sound to be set up along the half-wall (with an extension cord running from the house).

However, you are in charge! Feel free to make whatever executive decisions you need to ensure things run as smoothly as possible. Cathy and Cory, the Sunshine Mountain innkeepers, can answer any questions you have or help out with any of your needs.

After the ceremony, please grab Matt's iPod so you can hook it up to your system on the flagstone patio. Please start the playlist entitled: Reception Dinner. Use your judgment to determine how loud it should be.

Around 8 p.m., Matt and I will tell you it's time for our dance. You'll direct everyone to gather around the flagstone patio. The wedding party will get in a semi-circle around Matt and me, and we will look like we're about to do a serious dance. You'll say something cheesy like, "It's time for the couple's first dance." Then you'll press play on the Reception Dance playlist. The first song will be "Kiss" by Prince.

After that, people will be welcomed onto the dance floor for the party.

Thank you again for all your help, Nick!

Trying to think through the specific directions for each job can help you finalize a lot of little details. If you figure everything out in advance and clearly communicate it to those who are helping you, things should work smoothly during the event. (But even if they don't, you're going to enjoy yourself anyway!)

TAKING SHORTCUTS (ON THINGS THAT DON'T REALLY MATTER)

If at any point during your efforts to pull together a handcrafted, meaningful, and memorable celebration of love, commitment, and community you start to get stressed out about all you "have to" do, take a long hard look at your to-do list and take shortcuts wherever possible.

At first, it may seem like there isn't a single place to take a shortcut. Most likely, there is. Instead of taking a project to 100 percent, try stopping at 80 percent or, as with the handmade napkins for our wedding, 25 percent. Instead of sewing all the edges of our cloth napkins nicely and neatly, I cut them with pinking shears. Maybe that was only 15 percent?

"When you realize you want to spend the rest of your life with somebody, you want the rest of your life to start as soon as possible."

– Harry Burns (Billy Crystal), *When Harry Met Sally...*

But *it didn't matter*. People still had fun, and we were still married in the end. Plus, our sanity and our relationship were still intact—priceless.

CROSSING OFF NONESSENTIAL ITEMS

We crossed off a lot of to-do tasks recommended by the wedding industrial complex before we even started planning our wedding, and we continued to cross off items as our planning progressed. With some things, we simply realized that we didn't have the time, money, or desire to complete them. One such task was the scrapbook.

Our initial idea was to ask guests to contribute to some sort of scrapbook during the wedding (with notes, photos, and so on), but the $50 we allocated to the idea quickly got consumed by more pressing needs: alcohol and food. We knew we were going to take a group photo, including guests, after the wedding ceremony, so we would at least have a visual record of everyone in attendance. I also reminded myself of another useful mantra: "No matter what happens, we'll be married in the end—scrapbook or no scrapbook!"

Kristina, one of the designers and bloggers behind 100layercake.com, "had big, big plans for the . . . projects" she wanted to DIY for her wedding. "But as the months ticked by and the day grew closer," she realized that unless she planned to drive herself "to the very edge of sanity," she was going to have to cross things off the list. In the end, she learned an important lesson: "DIY doesn't mean doing everything yourself to the nth degree. It means crafting a meaningful celebration with the time and resources you have available. Most importantly, you want to feel great going into your big day, not exhausted and stressed. Sure, I was sad that a few major things I'd planned were missing, but *no one else* noticed. Our guests had a fantastic time, we had a fantastic time, and the important parts of the celebration were all in place."

DON'T LET YOUR WEDDING OVERSHADOW YOUR RELATIONSHIP

In *Sex and the City* (the movie), Carrie starts out with very practical aspirations for her wedding day. She even plans to wear a white pantsuit. Somewhere along the way, she gets caught up in the wedding industrial complex, and her wedding grows bigger and bigger. Then Big backs out of the wedding because he doesn't recognize her anymore.

With all the pressure we put on ourselves and the pressure from those around us, it can be easy to let the wedding overshadow the relationship. It's easy to get caught up in the mystique of the whole thing. It's got to be The Perfect Day. It's The Big Day. It's The Fairy Tale Ending. It's especially hard when everything you read or see about weddings fuels the fire.

It's hard to keep your eye on what is truly important about the event. It's a time to reconnect with family and friends and build new connections. It's a chance to set aside time to exalt love and express commitments. If we spend too much time obsessing about name cards or flower arrangements, we can lose sight of that. Two strategies for keeping your wedding planning in check:

- Cultivate yourself as a couple beyond your wedding. Throughout the wedding planning process, set aside plenty of time to do what you enjoy doing as a couple rather than spending all your free time working on seating charts or making playlists.
- Get advice from wedding veterans. When wedding details start to seem really important, chat with a friend or relative who is already married to get his or her perspective about what matters and what doesn't.

FAMILY CONFLICT

No matter how careful you are when you paint a room in your house, you end up with paint splatters somewhere. It just happens—despite your best intentions. I think of family conflict during the wedding planning process in the same way. It's pretty much inevitable since there's so much going on emotionally.

First, there's the symbolic nature of the whole affair. You're officially transferring from one family to another (even if you've already been on your own for a long time). Then there's the whole social pressure piece. Everyone has his or her own cultural baggage about what makes a *real* wedding. Other times, preexisting family drama gets exacerbated.

To further complicate matters, there could be conflicting impulses. On the one hand, you might want your wedding to represent who you and your partner are as a new family. On the other hand, you might want to honor the family you've come from. Sometimes those goals are aligned, and sometimes they are not.

As you navigate the fluctuating waters of wedding planning in the context of family conflict, keep the following tips in mind:

- Be patient with your family. Weddings are an incredibly symbolic rite of passage. If your family is freaking out about something inane, like chair covers, it might actually be about something deeper—such as mourning how quickly time has passed. Have empathy and understanding for all the emotions that play out during the wedding planning process.
- Put your foot down when you need to. Sometimes conflict and wedding drama are about something else entirely, such as your family members feeling like *your* wedding represents *them*. They might want to spend more money, make the event more formal, or make choices that reflect their tastes and preferences to impress people. When that's happening, it's perfectly acceptable to put your foot down. It is *your* wedding, and it should reflect you and your partner. Your married family members already had chances to plan their own weddings! This issue gets complicated, however, if you've chosen to accept their financial contributions to the event.
- Compromise when it makes sense. Sometimes it makes sense to listen to a family member's request if implementing it wouldn't bother you too much. Just be careful because compromising on something that seems small in the beginning (such as the formality of the venue choice) can affect a ton of other decisions later on down the line. Also, it's easy to make little compromises here and there and then suddenly realize that you're planning someone else's dream wedding.
- Keep the lines of communication open. Good communication is a solid part of resolving conflict. It can be so easy to vent your family frustrations to your partner rather than discussing the issues head-on with your family. No matter how hard it is, it needs to be done. It's usually the only way to handle conflict maturely and productively.
- Remember that you are setting precedents. As easy as it can be to compromise here or there on different aspects of your wedding, remember that the patterns you establish with your family now won't stop at your wedding. They will carry over into other big milestones,

"Unless you plan to elope secretly in the dark of night, or have planned a small intimate wedding, you may soon find your wedding plans escalating out of control. This one-sentence wedding mantra may be helpful. Recite it to yourselves in those moments when everyone about you seems to be going crazy with the planning details: The point of the wedding is to celebrate our love and make a public commitment to each other for life. Everything else is extra."

– Lilo and Gerard Leeds, ***Wonderful Marriage: A Guide to Building a Great Relationship that Will Last***

such as having children (if you choose to). For example, you might want to give birth in a birthing center, while your family might prefer you to be in a hospital. Weddings are a good opportunity to show your family that—while you value their input, advice, counsel, experiences, and perspectives—you ultimately need to make decisions that reflect who you are and what you value.

Stephanie, a full-time student in Maryland, and her partner, William, decided to sidestep the wedding planning process and a celebration full of conflict by eloping. She said, "No one is invited because of the abundance of drama. It's our day, and we don't want to be mediators."

Allyson, a teacher from Virginia, and her partner took the opposite approach. They said, "We finally realized that it was OUR day and that if we wanted to do things differently, then that was what was going to happen. We eventually just had to tell our families that we weren't going to do things the way they wanted because it didn't reflect who we were and that it was just too bad. After we talked with them, they were more understanding. It was hard, but we just had to shut out some of the comments they made about things. In the end, everyone enjoyed the wedding."

Even though wedding planning would be a heck of a lot easier if you didn't have to deal with family conflict, you have to prepare yourself for its inevitability. That way, you'll be ready when it does happen or pleasantly surprised when it doesn't.

EMOTIONAL GAMUT

When I was little, I used to throw up the night before my birthday due to sheer excitement. As I grew older, my stomach problems continued. I had an upset stomach the morning I started teaching third grade in rural Louisiana and before random Internet dates several years ago.

And less than a week before my wedding, I was plagued with stomach problems again. I couldn't tell if I was anxious about the wedding, the move back to Texas, buying a house, or the new job.

I think I was most nervous about whether or not we would be able to pull off a $2,000 wedding. During the planning process, we made so many assumptions:

- We assumed we could make a wedding meaningful and memorable with sincerity rather than money.
- We assumed that guests would feel more involved and connected to the wedding if they were responsible for making it happen.
- We assumed that doing it all ourselves would help us truly immerse ourselves in the experience.
- We assumed that all the systems we set up would work like clockwork so that we could truly enjoy the experience in a stress-free way.
- We assumed that we had put enough structures in place to help our friends and family get to know each other.
- We assumed that we had enough food, that it would taste good, and that it wouldn't make our guests sick.

I'm surprised the stomach problems lasted only a day!

Whenever we go through major life transitions, it's completely normal to experience emotions that run the gamut. Wedding planning is no exception. The trick is to be prepared to experience all sorts of emotions and to be patient with ourselves as we sort them all out.

IDEAS FOR NEXT STEPS

- Create a detailed wedding agenda that allows you to visualize the flow of your wedding, clarify what still needs to be decided or done, and communicate with those who are helping you.
- Finalize your to-bring list. Read over your detailed agenda and visualize everything that's going on and what you need to do to make each moment happen (working backward from the end state). Write your lists in a centralized place (and triple-check them).
- Remind yourself that your marriage is more important than your wedding.
- Create detailed task descriptions and instructions for anyone who is helping you. That way, your helpers won't have to ask clarifying questions on the day of your wedding.
- Take shortcuts whenever possible to preserve your sanity.
- Take a hard look at your remaining to-do list and cross off everything that's not absolutely essential. You want to be in a relaxed frame of mind, as much as is possible, as you go into your wedding day.
- Have fun and remember that no matter what happens, you'll be married in the end!

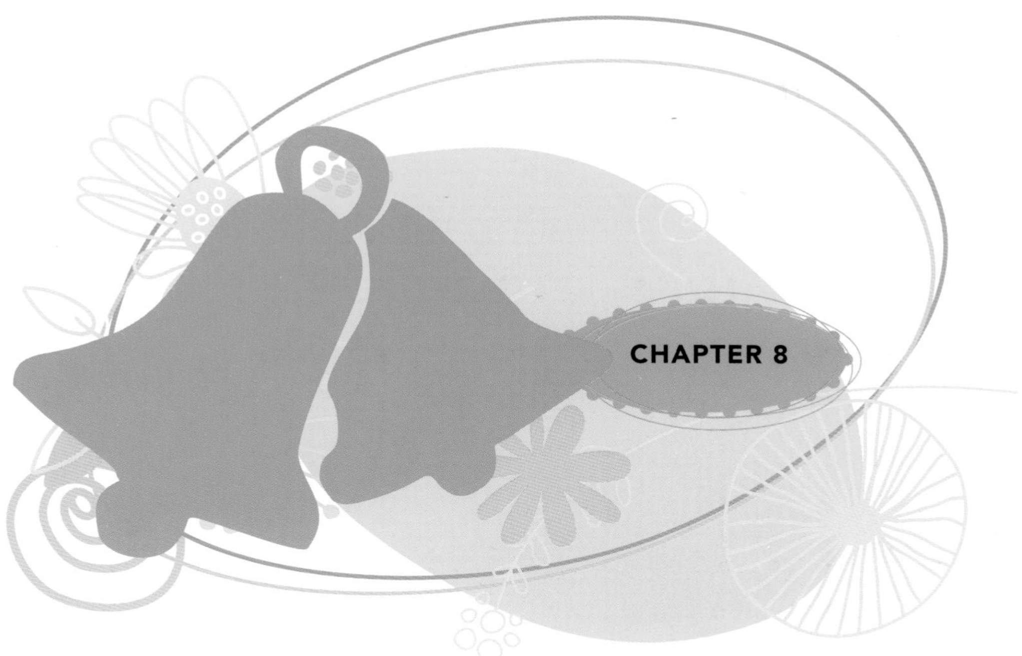

The Wedding

It's time to put all the planning behind you. You've worked through vision setting, the big decisions, spreading the word, ceremony planning, all the other details, and the final stretch. Now is the time to take a deep breath and let it all go. Your wedding is here. Immerse yourself in the experience and enjoy it to the fullest extent possible.

OUR STORY

DAY 1: WEDNESDAY

Matt and I packed the car and left Denver to head to Sunshine Mountain Lodge. When we arrived, we unloaded all our food and sundry supplies. Then we met up with my family at Meeker Park Lodge. We went high into the tundra, picnicked on a mountaintop, and slid down a snowy hill on our butts. I was with my Floridian brother as he experienced snow for the first time.

That afternoon, Matt and I met up with his mom where she was staying: Lake Mary's Lodge. Matt's mom treated me to a relaxing manicure and pedicure at the resort's spa. Then we dined together on the premises.

DAY 2: THURSDAY

I enjoyed fresh blueberries and strawberries with Matt's mom and then headed to Meeker Park Lodge for some horseback riding on the edge of Rocky Mountain National Park with my family. After a delicious lunch on the porch of a café, I went back to Sunshine Mountain Lodge and finished some small preparations, such as ironing our wedding clothes and setting up the name tags for the Friday night welcome picnic. My college friend Marsha and her husband arrived, and we began hanging white Christmas lights (lent to us by Cathy and Cory) along the flagstone patio to ensure we had enough light for night dancing. We played a few games and then trekked to Estes Park for dinner when our hunger got the best of us.

DAY 3: FRIDAY

We ate a yummy homemade breakfast of cobbler, blueberry muffins, and fresh fruit on the flagstone patio for a leisurely two hours. Then we finished hanging the rest of the lights and began preparation for the welcome picnic. Matt and I made and decorated a cookie cake for his brother's birthday and made a chocolate-cherry dessert. We also mixed some iced tea and lemonade.

People started arriving in the early afternoon. We ate at the make-your-own-sandwich bar, which also had chips and watermelon. People congregated in different areas to talk and connect. Some moseyed up to the fire to cook s'mores, while others found their way to the hot tub. Around 8:00 p.m., we had a swing dancing lesson on the back patio.

DAY 4: SATURDAY

We lingered over fruit, homemade scones, and frittata. Then the wedding party headed to Meeker Park for the rehearsal. We ran through the ceremony twice and then found a shady patch in which to practice our rehearsal dance. Next we headed up to Mary's Lake Lodge to attend a luncheon that Matt's family had planned for our families and the wedding party. When we returned to Sunshine Mountain Lodge, we started preparation for the reception dinner. One crew worked on the fajitas; another worked on the seven-layer dip; my crew worked on the guacamole; and others worked on the salsa. There were about fifteen of us in all, chopping and talking. Some people helped Cathy and Cory move tables. Various friends stopped by to ask what we needed help with. I asked my friend Laura to hike through the woods around our cabins to collect wildflowers for my bouquet.

After getting ready among friends, Matt and I hopped in our car and drove to the ceremony site. We mingled with our guests as they arrived. After they finished arriving and received programs and root beer (or bottled water), we started a special song that signaled to members of the wedding party that it was time to make their way to the front.

Right when the ceremony started, our dog, Hoss, who was standing in the wedding party with Matt's brother, started throwing up all the grass he had eaten. Matt's brother quickly walked him away. I felt awkward with my hands at my side and realized I had forgotten my bouquet. I sprinted back to the table to retrieve my wayward flowers. Those things didn't feel like flaws, however. They felt like well-timed bits of comic relief.

The ceremony went exactly as we wanted. The five people who spoke on our behalf (with complete autonomy to craft their speeches and surprise us during the ceremony) said beautiful and different things. The tree planting and quilt wrapping were exactly the symbolic gestures we wanted them to be, and our vows had the intended effect of making people laugh and cry.

After the ceremony, the photography session was quick and painless. Then we followed our guests to the reception site. Matt and I had alone time during the drive. Once we arrived at Sunshine Mountain Lodge, the reception was in full swing. Tables were set up in a grove of trees, and people were helping themselves to drinks and appetizers. I had some seven-layer dip, guacamole, salsa, and nacho cheese. I couldn't believe the $1-per-bag chips we got at Sam's Club were actually tasty. Our friends worked on the fajitas and delivered up a seriously delicious spread. We didn't have any problem getting eighty people through a two-sided buffet line. The quality of the sound system that our friend-in-a-band provided was so superior that my friend Jamie said, "I tried to find where the live music was coming from!"

Matt and I were able to chat with our friends and family as we ate. After dinner, we had a brief cake ceremony. We decided not to make the cake ceremony all about us and instead used the time to thank our friends and family for making the event possible. Then our guests helped themselves to six different cake options. Many guests opted for small slices of several different cakes.

After cake, we called everyone to the flagstone patio for our "first dance." Our wedding party stood around us in a semicircle and pretended to watch. Our friend announced our first dance and started the song. Then the entire wedding party broke into a dance to "Kiss" by Prince. When the general dancing started, several guests joined us on the makeshift dance floor. (During one song, Matt's brother, John, stripped off some clothes and did a bit of a lap dance on his cousin. Even my grandparents cracked up.)

The patio started to slightly resemble a frat party, with keg stands and stripping. Some guests played word games in the living room, while others hung out around the campfire. Some headed for the hot tub.

Cathy, the innkeeper, joined us on the dance floor for a while. She and Cory even gave us a gift. I danced a lot, played a game, stopped by the fire, got in the hot tub, and mainly just chatted with my close friends. What a night!

DAY 5: SUNDAY

We started the day with another leisurely homemade breakfast. Then people packed up and started trekking back to the airport. My friends Brent and Laura and I went for a hike in Rocky Mountain National Park. We picnicked and hiked and talked. Afterward I headed to Mary's Lake Lodge to nap at Matt's parents' place. When I awoke, I snacked on cake and looked at photos and video from the wedding.

DAY 6: MONDAY

Hoss and I headed to Sunshine Mountain Lodge one more time. Cathy and Cory treated us to a free homemade breakfast, and I enjoyed hanging out with Jeff and Paul, two of my closest friends from college.

LETTING GO AND ENJOYING YOURSELF

At this point in the process, you've invested considerable time, energy, and emotion into your wedding. It's only natural to feel like there's so much at stake! But it's time to let go. You've done your best to organize the inputs to the best of your ability, but you can't control the outputs. You can make plans and double-check lists, but you can't determine how the wedding unfolds on the day of. While it's true that the more effort you put into planning upfront, the more likely the wedding will turn out well, there are no guarantees. Do your best and then let go. The best part of letting go is that it frees you to enjoy yourself to the greatest extent possible.

As much as humanly possible, make sure your wedding doesn't just fly by. You want to fully engage yourself in it and soak up the celebration. You can do this by reminding yourself to:

- Stop and celebrate all you've accomplished. Pulling together a wedding—no matter how big or small—is a major feat. Take a second to pat yourself on the back (or pour yourself and your partner a glass of champagne or schedule a couple's massage). It's easy to focus on what you could have or should have done. Don't do that do yourself. Focus on everything you *did* do. Celebrate the positive and be proud of your accomplishments.
- Embrace the space between what happens and how you respond to what happens. You have done your very best to plan your best wedding. Now that your wedding is here, you aren't in control of what happens. You are in complete control of how you respond to what happens, however. If something doesn't go according to plan, let go and focus on the joy. The mishap will make a good story. And, most importantly, no matter what happens, you'll still be married in the end.

IDEAS FOR NEXT STEPS

- Write a letter to yourself before your wedding, to help you stay calm and grounded when the day arrives. Read the letter in the days leading up to your wedding. Then give it to a trusted friend or family member to read it to you on your wedding day. Use the space on the next page to compose your letter.
- Have fun and bask in the fact that you planned your very best wedding and soon you will be officially united with your beloved!

Letter to Myself

Write a letter to yourself, to read or have read to you on your wedding day. What do you want to celebrate? What do you want to remind yourself of?

The Ever After

You are now pronounced husband and wife (or wife and wife, or husband and husband, or partner and partner). Commence with the shouts of joy. To wrap things up, we talk about avoiding a postwedding meltdown, sending out thank-you cards, dealing with the last name dilemma, and—most importantly—maintaining your marriage.

OUR STORY

On the way home from our wedding, we stopped and picked up a moving van. That afternoon, we packed the whole thing. The next day, we drove all day and then got stuck trying to back the moving van into a parking spot at a hotel. The following day we finished the rest of the drive to Houston, drove to the bank to deposit our wedding money, got a cashier's check for almost every penny in our bank account, drove straight to a title company, and signed all the papers. We moved into our house that evening. If we had spent any more money on our wedding, we wouldn't have been able to afford our new house.

Despite the stress of planning a wedding, moving a thousand or so miles, and starting new jobs all in the same summer, Matt and I settled into married life well. We tried to write our thank-you cards as quickly as possible. We sent them to everyone who attended the wedding, not just people who gave us tangible gifts. We wanted to show appreciation for everyone's presence.

The front of the card included a collage of pictures from the wedding. I honestly cried as I wrote some of the cards. I was so touched by our friends' willingness to help out.

I was much more relaxed and sensible about the thank-you cards than I had been about the invitations. When I worked on the invitations, I was neurotic and insecure. I read each message multiple times to make sure I hadn't made a mistake. I tripled-checked the invitations for smudges. With the thank-you cards, I simply wrote each message, read over it once, and sent it.

It makes me wonder if a special phenomenon exists. It's as if we see the world through a different lens when we're planning a wedding. This lens has a tendency to make us more neurotic, more obsessed, more insecure, and more anxious, which is the exact opposite of what you actually want to feel on your wedding day.

Matt and I went on a "honeymoon" sailing adventure around the Greek islands (with a pitstop in Paris) a year after our wedding, but we called it our annual adventure because we like to go on a big trip every year.

As for dealing with the last name situation, Matt and I definitely faced a dilemma: I didn't want to change mine, and he didn't want to change his. I didn't want to change my name for several reasons, namely:

- By the time I got married, I had already been Sara Cotner for thirty years. I'd made many contacts throughout those years, and I didn't want to make it difficult for people (primarily former students) to find me. Plus, my name is a huge part of my identity.
- I'm not a huge fan of hyphenation. I find it cumbersome. I totally support people who choose that route for themselves because I think it's a good

compromise and I like the philosophy behind it. I just don't personally like it for practical reasons.

- I don't like the patriarchal tradition of women giving up their last names when they get married.
- I like my last name. If I didn't like it, I would most likely have ignored my previous three reasons and just changed my name to Matt's (Bradford).

I was fine keeping my last name and was relieved to not have to deal with the hassle of legally changing my name during the wedding planning process. Now, years after our wedding, I'm starting to think about hyphenating my name. I just gave birth to our son, Henry, and we decided to hyphenate his name to represent the blending of two different families. Since he's Henry Cotner-Bradford, Matt and I are considering taking Cotner-Bradford as our common last name.

Fortunately, I didn't experience any sadness or disappointment after our wedding. It was just the opposite! I was incredibly proud of us for pulling off the best wedding for us (under budget, no less!), and my confidence was bolstered. These days, I'm busy with other crazy schemes and still use backward planning from the vision to the smaller steps to make things happen. I thank my wedding planning experience for proving that anything is possible with the power of partnership, persistence, optimism, hard work, resourcefulness, and organization.

AVOIDING A POST-WEDDING MELTDOWN

A common thing happens in K–12 schools. When Thanksgiving, winter, or spring break starts, teachers get sick. It's definitely an annoying pattern. It's as if your body holds everything in and prevents itself from getting sick while you're working. But once you relax, it's all over. Your body finally lets itself get sick.

The same thing happened to my friend Camella after her wedding and to her friend Wiley after her wedding. Camella even had to go to the hospital to get examined. Because Camella's wedding was three months before mine, I had time to learn from her experience. I tried to make sure that I proactively dealt with the stress of planning a wedding.

Ironically, the busier and more stressed we get, the less time we have for the things that help us alleviate our stress. Case in point: exercise. Exercise makes me feel better. Yet when my to-do list stretches out the door, I have a hard time making time for exercise. (I also tend to prioritize other things above exercise because they are less active and just easier.)

I'm pretty convinced I was able to avoid a postwedding breakdown by proactively dealing with my stress. Here are my two recommended strategies:

- Make time for things you *have* to do (exercising, cleaning the house, cooking regular meals, and so on) to decrease your stress.
- Make time for things you *want* to do (reading, going for a walk, catching up with friends, watching a movie).

Some people get depressed after a wedding. The wedding is over. The months and months of planning (for most people) are now done. Everyone has gone home. Your big project has come to completion. People who let wedding planning become their primary focus for many months are most susceptible to this kind of letdown. I avoided depression by occupying myself with other projects that built community and connection: a community time bank, a retro prom birthday party, dinner parties with friends.

Think about which part of the wedding planning you truly enjoyed and build more of that into your life. Maybe you need more parties with friends or family? Maybe you need to start making and selling crafts? Maybe you need to take a cake-decorating class?

LAST NAME DILEMMA

As with every other part of the wedding planning process, you have options when it comes to figuring out what to do about the last name situation:

- You can change your last name to your partner's.
- Your partner can change his or her last name to yours.
- You can both hyphenate your last names.
- You can make up a new last name, perhaps by blending your names or coming up with something entirely new.

Every couple has to figure out what makes sense for them. Erin, who got married in Massachusetts in 2009, said, "I never wanted to change my last name, but my partner really wanted us to share a family name and suggested we even come up with our own name. We decided to both hyphenate, which felt right. I didn't expect to, but I love that we have signified the creation and creativity of our own family that way. And we'll let our kids figure out what to do with all those hyphens when they get married!"

Katy, on the other hand, changed her name to her partner's. She "was not that attached" to her name, and she likes tradition. She also thinks "it is important for the kids for everyone in the family to have the same last name."

Anna and Braden decided to keep their own names. Anna explained, "My mother kept her last name . . . so I didn't think it was weird at all to keep mine. Of course, there are people on either side who are distraught by this, but there was really no way I was going to change it. I think weddings should be celebrations of love and community, not a merger of businesses. I feel really good about keeping my name and will handle the baby naming problems when we get there."

The decision about what to do with the last name is a very personal one. The best you can do is make the decision that feels right to you and your partner.

MAINTAINING YOUR MARRIAGE

Most wedding talk revolves around the details: invitations, cake, shoes, hair, nails. Detailed calendars ("One Year Out"; "Eleven Months and Counting") provide list upon list of all the details you have to attend to in order to make your day special. Talking about the details can be fun, but they are the trees. Remember that there's a whole forest out there. The forest is the marriage.

Here are a few tips for building a successful relationship (culled from our trials and tribulations):

DIVIDE HOUSEHOLD CHORES EQUITABLY

When Matt and I first moved in together, we made a list of everything that needed to get done on a weekly basis (cleaning the kitchen, laundry, vacuuming, cleaning the bathroom, wiping down tabletops, mowing the lawn, putting away dishes, taking out the trash, taking out the compost, watering the plants, shaking out the rugs). We divided all the tasks into four categories. The first two categories are things that Matt always does (mowing the lawn and putting away the dishes) and things I always do (laundry and taking out the compost). We divided the rest of the chores into two equal lists: Laborer 1 and Laborer 2. On a weekly basis, Matt and I alternate who takes on which role. That way, we don't build up any resentment about what's fair or not; we're always switching back and forth. Plus, it helps liven up the chore routine (at least a minuscule amount).

COME UP WITH A FINANCIAL PLAN

If you were to do an informal interview with married couples and ask them the number-one cause of their fights, a high percentage would probably say money. It makes sense. Different people have different approaches to money. For example, one parent in my family is a saver; the other buys plastic, blow-up football figures for the lawn just because. Matt and I are both savers. But we still had to come up with a plan for our joint financial approach. We had to sit down and talk through how we would merge finances in the most agreeable, amenable way. In the end, we came up with a system of multiple accounts. Both of our paychecks go into a centralized account, from which we pay our common bills: mortgage, groceries, entertainment. We also use the money to build our savings accounts to pay for home improvements, a car, the baby, vacations, and retirement. Finally, we each get $70 once a month to spend on whatever suits our individual fancies. If he wants to buy a blow-up football figure with his own money, I won't argue. (The argument will come if he actually puts it in the front yard.)

FIGURE OUT YOUR LANGUAGES OF LOVE

According to *The Five Love Languages* by Gary Chapman, there are five distinct ways to show love to our partners. If we aren't consciously aware of how our partner prefers to be loved, we can inadvertently create conflict by failing to meet his or her needs. Here are the five love languages, according to Chapman:

- Words of affirmation. You feel loved when people tell you or write to you about why they appreciate and love you.
- Quality time. You feel loved when people make time to hang out with you.
- Physical touch. You feel loved when people hug, cuddle, and are physically affectionate with you.
- Acts of service. You feel loved when people do things that are typically your responsibility to show their love for you (get you a glass of water, make the bed).
- Receiving gifts. You feel loved when someone cares enough to think about you and express his or her love through tangible gifts.

COMMIT TO SOLVING CONFLICT

When Matt and I are tired and arguing, we tend to go around in circles. It's quite frustrating. He'll state his argument. I'll argue with his argument. He'll argue with my argument. Sometimes we argue about nothing. When that happens, we're pretty good about cutting ourselves off by saying, "We're both tired; let's go to sleep." Sometimes, though, we argue about real stuff—real frustrations or resentment. To reach resolution, when an argument goes around and around, one person stops and asks, "What do you need me to do so you can

feel better about this?" The person lists his or her needs, and the other person tries very hard to commit to them. Then we reverse the process.

ADMIT WHEN YOU'RE WRONG

For a lot of people, it's not easy to admit when we're wrong (about big or small things). Being honest about your wrongness goes a long way in terms of building trust in a relationship.

BE GOOD TO EACH OTHER, EVEN IN THE MOST STRESSFUL MOMENTS

In the first six months of marriage, Matt and I weathered a hurricane that caused almost a $1,000 in damage to our new house and that completely destroyed our close friends' house. Then both our cars were stolen from our driveway while we slept. Then Matt's wallet was stolen. It's easy for stress to invite conflict into a relationship. In stressful moments, it's important to realize that we can't control the ups and downs. However, we can control our reactions to those ups and downs. In anxiety-ridden moments, we can stop and say, "At least we have each other." When the world around us is unsettled, we need to keep the center stable. Fighting or getting frustrated with each other only makes the situation worse.

SAY THANK YOU—A LOT!

When you live with someone day in and day out (whether it's a family member, a roommate, or a significant other), it's easy to take that person for granted. The nice things he or she does for you or your home become commonplace. They become expected. One thing I've learned from living with Matt is how good it feels to be thanked for these things (and to thank others for these things). For example, Matt certainly doesn't need to thank me for doing my half of the chores. It's my responsibility! But when he thanks me for it, he's acknowledging that he noticed my effort—that my contribution is important to him. He's communicating, "Hey, I'm glad you help maintain a system of equity in our relationship. I appreciate your reliability."

PLAN DATE NIGHTS

It's easy to get caught up in the day-to-day responsibilities of adulthood. Intentionally setting aside time for dates can be a great way to have fun and to stay connected.

SURPRISE EACH OTHER

Matt and I certainly don't do this as much as we did when we were dating, but we still try to leave spontaneous notes and small gifts (handmade and store-bought) for each other.

Our Celebration of Love July 2008

DIY Project 10:

PRACTICAL SCRAPBOOK

Hooray for your new family! If you're looking for a no-hassle, sustainable way to chronicle your life together, this scrapbook project might be the answer. It's a simple project. You don't need to be a perfectionist to do it. The scrapbook is also quick and easy to update.

MATERIALS

A thick binder (the thicker it is, the more years it will fit) with a clear plastic cover on the outside

Decorative paper to slip into the outside of the binder cover

Page protectors

Acid-free cardstock

Archival double-sided tape

Printed photos

Tip: Old maps or calendars are excellent sources for decorative paper to slip into the binder cover.

DIRECTIONS

1. Print photos. (I use an online photo printing service that mails photos directly to my house.)
2. Arrange photos on cardstock. (I can fit two to three pictures per page, depending on the arrangement.)
3. Use double-sided tape to secure the photos.
4. Jot down a little note about each photo.
5. Insert the cardstock into page protectors and snap them into your binder.

MY WISH FOR YOU

When I look back at the pictures from our wedding or pass by our wedding quilt on the end of our bed, I am still overwhelmed by such appreciation and by the wedding we were able to pull off. It prioritized community, connection, commitment, and fun. It showcased our values: handcrafted, eco-friendly, and budget-minded.

I wasn't stressed during the ceremony because I was excited to share it with our friends and family, and I was close to most of the people in the audience. The reception didn't fly by in a blur because I didn't have to do the "meet and greet" thing. I had spent time with people at breakfast, made guacamole with them in the kitchen, hung out with them in the hot tub, and ridden on horses and hiked with them days before the wedding. I didn't have any stressful interactions with vendors because most of the vendors were our friends.

It was the perfect wedding *for us*.

As a bonus, during the wedding planning process, I practiced and honed many valuable life skills, such as dreaming big, being myself despite others' disapproval, taking a big project and breaking it into smaller chunks, talking myself down from moments of irrationality and insecurity, and collaborating with my partner to create the kind of life we could only begin to imagine. After the wedding, I picked up my little backpack of skills and carried it to my next endeavor: creating a time exchange system in my neighborhood. And my next endeavor: creating an online course about preparing your mind, body, and life for pregnancy. And my current endeavor: starting a national network of high-performing, authentic Montessori schools in diverse communities. I'm indebted to my little wedding for giving me the confidence to dwell in possibility, make a plan, and then make it happen.

Here's my wish for all of you who are planning a wedding: May you and your partner create the best possible wedding for you. Figure out what you want—what you really, really want your wedding to be. Then make it happen, regardless of the influence other people try to exert over you and regardless of anyone's skepticism or judgment.

After all, the wedding industrial complex is right about one thing:

*it is **your** day.*

APPENDIX:

Meet Kindred Spirits

Allison Campbell is pursuing her master's degree in climate change and energy policy in northern California. She enjoys playing with her dog, baking cookies, and thinking about ways to encourage equity in the world without neglecting ecology. In 2009 she and her husband, Ryan, were married on the equinox (in honor of equality in marriage) at a summer camp in Oregon. They walked down the aisle together (an old Irish tradition), ro-sham-bo'd to decide who would say their vows first, and enjoyed the help of their friends and family in decorating the main cabin for their reception. Allison's writings about crafting their wedding (and marriage) can be found under the pseudonym Bearcub on weddingbee.com.

Erin Blache-Cohen is a mental health therapist who currently works with children and families. After grad school in Boston, marriage on the Cape, and an extended honeymoon in Southeast Asia, Erin and her husband, Brandon, headed to Pittsburgh, Pennsylvania, to plant some roots. They dig exploring the food, art, music, and fun of Brandon's hometown when they are not engrossed in home DIY projects (these days: trying to not lose their savings and sanity while finishing the basement). Their family includes Mo and Pikku, dog and cat, respectively. Erin hopes to include some urban chickens soon too.

Christa L. Crabill and Brian have been together for over ten years and were married on September 5, 2010. After moving multiple times for college and work, a few months before they got married Christa and Brian moved back to the small town where Christa grew up. They live in the home her grandparents built. Christa loves spending as much time as possible with family and friends, cooking, baking, and gardening during the summer. She is a huge sports fan and always looks forward to creating new experiences with loved ones.

Andrea Elliott lives with her husband in Syracuse, New York, in a cute little house with a backyard just big enough for playing Wiffle Ball. Someday she wants to own a coffee shop or a gym and live in an old farmhouse in the country. She misses being a kid, and doesn't think kids these days spend enough time playing outdoors. She's not ashamed to shop at thrift stores or flea markets and has made a pledge to buy only secondhand and handmade for a year. She enjoys married life tremendously and hopes to start a family within the next couple of years.

Sarah Gillepsie was raised in New Jersey and lived and worked in Washington, D.C., for ten years before moving to Boston with her husband, Adam. She currently attends Andover Newton Theological School and is pursuing ordination as a Unitarian Universalist minister. She is passionate about being a religious liberal and will spend the rest of her life having conversations about what that means. When she's not reading or writing about theology, she enjoys knitting, bread-making, music, and sports. Above all, Sarah relishes time spent with all the different people she calls family.

Jocelyn Godwin is an artist, lover of words, wife, and teacher in the making. She lives in the foggy city of Saint John, New Brunswick, and studies at the University of New Brunswick. She is proud to spend her life with her nerdy, computer-loving husband. They were high school sweethearts who sealed the deal in June 2010 at a beloved summer cottage. Without the help of unconventional wedding blogs such as 2000dollarwedding.com, they surely would have lost their heads before the wedding took place.

Liz Grotyohann lives in Portland, Oregon, where she runs a small design and web development firm, Super Runaway, with her husband, Jeff. Married in 2009, Liz and Jeff enjoy each other's company enough to spend 90 percent of their time together, which seems like a pretty good testament to the institution of marriage. Their wedding was cheap, green, nontraditional, emotional, and superfun—their friends and family are still talking about it. In fact, more than a few friends have thanked Liz and Jeff for being an example as they planned their own, more meaningful, less commercial, weddings.

Born and raised Minnesotans, **Molly and Aaron Heit** are now living and working as science teachers in rural Mississippi through the Mississippi Teacher Corps. They hope to one day open an early childhood development and community educational center that strives to empower the next generation to live their lives fully, in a sustainable way. Molly and Aaron's DIY, budget-friendly wedding took place on an educational farm in Minnesota, where they were surrounded by family, friends, and nature. They love spending their free time in the outdoors, biking, kayaking, gardening, and crafting.

Ivy Hest lives in Boston but grew up in southern Florida. She works as a community organizer, helping low-income seniors to fight for their rights. In her spare time, she sings in an a cappella group and dances. She met her husband, Seth, in the Jewish Organizing Initiative, a yearlong fellowship on community organizing. He hails from Troy, New York, and works as a training coordinator for a labor union. They got married on September 17, 2011, at the World Fellowship Retreat Center in Conway, New Hampshire.

Maureen Hodson was raised in New England but has adopted northern California as her home. She lives with her husband, David, her brand-new daughter, and a grumpy old cat. Maureen and David married in 2009 in a casual outdoor ceremony in the Wine Country. She is currently learning to juggle motherhood and a busy and fulfilling environmental litigation practice. When she's not working, she's raising her daughter the Montessori way, hiking the beautiful trails of Marin County with her family, and enjoying all the benefits of California living (especially the year-round farmers' markets and local wine).

Megan Howarth lives in Montreal, Quebec, with her husband, Peter, a guitar player and singer, and their son, Dylan. Her backyard wedding was a blast, and although there was no set budget and a few dramatic bridal moments took place, it was a relaxed, casual, and intimate day. She was married a few houses down the street from her childhood home, and the following week, neighbors were still talking about the great music they heard from their porches that night. After getting married and having a baby, Megan became a birth doula and now helps support other women during pregnancy and birth. Her website is meganthedoula.com.

Zinaida M. is an artsy, outdoorsy, chocolate-abusing travel-holic who lives in Chapel Hill, North Carolina, with her husband, hedgehog, and cat. Putting aside the vast majority of the wedding budget for an epic sailing honeymoon in Greece, she got creative making wedding decor with items acquired cheaply or for no cost. With an eye for style and a sense of adventure, Zinaida and her husband treated their friends and families to a tasteful yet fitting weekend-long wedding celebration in the mountains of North Carolina.

Anna-Marie McLemore is a Lambda Literary Fellow in fiction. Her work appears in ten Cleis Press anthologies, in *CRATE* magazine's "cratelit," and on the website of the Huntington-USC Institute on California and the West. Her husband, Jo Michael, a Colorado native, is a third-year law student and an activist for LGBT rights. They met in Los Angeles when Anna-Marie was seventeen and Jo was eighteen. They currently live in northern California.

Marina Moses Shuman lives with her husband, Zack, and her baby, Rosa, in Portland, Oregon, fifteen blocks from the park in which they got married. She works at a local nonprofit helping people with terminal illnesses and enjoys playing the ukulele and baking bread.

Sebrina Parker Schultz is a young newlywed nonhousewife. While she enjoys cooking daily meals, the cleaning and laundry get left to her husband. They are both part-time freelancers and full-time Christian ministry volunteers. They live as simply and cheaply as possible to prepare for a year of travel.

Sherry Petersik and her hubby, John, are full-time home bloggers at younghouselove.com. They started the blog in 2007 as a personal DIY diary. It now attracts more than 4 million hits a month. They've been featured on *The Nate Berkus Show*, HGTV, and CNN, and in the *New York Times*. They juggle everything from kitchen and bathroom gut jobs to a regular column in a national magazine—with a toddler and a nine-pound Chihuahua as their trusty assistants.

After growing up in Massachusetts, **Elizabeth Schroeder** spent four years earning a history degree at the University of Dayton. Between communal roommate dinners and late-night library sessions, she met her husband, Craig, who was studying to become a civil engineer. Their courtship continued beyond graduation as she pursued a master's degree in public history at IUPUI and he began working in Cincinnati. They were married in 2010 in Craig's hometown of Ottawa. Elizabeth fills her spare time with dance classes and baking, while Craig prefers to brew his own beer. They live with their dog, Turk, and cat, Kitty.

Heather Shoberg is a small-town girl from Colorado who moved to Minnesota to follow her future husband. She enjoys photography and gardening as well as traveling with her husband to random destinations and attractions. They live with two cats, with the intention of growing their family, returning to Colorado, and finding a way to continue traveling to random locations around the United States and eventually the globe.

Allyson Speake grew up in rural New Hampshire but now lives with her husband; her newborn daughter, Avalea Grace; and two cats on Free Spirit Farm in the Shenandoah Valley of Virginia. She enjoys gardening, painting, baking bread, and selling homemade and natural cleaning products at the local farmers' market on weekends. After teaching for three years, she is currently enjoying time at home with her daughter. When she is not snuggling with Avalea, she is busy making her specialty, black currant jam, for the next farmers' market.

Gretchen Taylor lives in Noblesville, Indiana, with her husband, Andrew, along with their dog and two cats. She teaches English to at-risk high school students and loves the challenge of interesting them in grammar, literature, and the like. When she's not teaching, she spends her time reading (both books and blogs), knitting, scrapbooking, and blogging sporadically at www.notenoughdevotion.blogspot.com. When planning their wedding, the couple made sure to include personal and meaningful touches. They chose to get married on September 11 to honor Andrew's mother, who passed away on that date in 2005. They used kissing Dutch people as their cake topper because they met at Hope College in Holland, Michigan. Since their wedding two and a half years ago, they have bought a house, honeymooned in Maine, and enjoyed many other adventures together.

After bouncing between the East Coast and the West Coast for many years, **Victoria Tan** now resides in beautiful Vancouver, British Columbia, with her husband, Joe. She hopes to make the world a more equitable place by promoting literacy and bridging the digital divide. She is currently working toward an MLIS at the University of British Columbia. She embraces the simple things in life: reading a good book; cooking and savoring a meal of seasonal, locally grown ingredients; making and sending handwritten cards; enjoying a cup of tea; volunteering with friends; and playing piano-guitar duets with Joe.

Dan Upham has visited the highest and lowest points in the continental United States within the same twelve-hour time span, performed stand-up comedy in numerous New York

City clubs, and run the 2011 New York Marathon. By day he's a writer for the Environmental Defense Fund. Virginia Sole-Smith is a journalist whose work has appeared in more than forty publications, from *Parents* to the *New York Times*. In 2009–2010, Virginia chronicled her adventures in beauty school at beautyschooledproject.com in an effort to understand women's relationship to beauty; she also got really good at eyebrow waxing. Dan and Virginia live in the Hudson Valley with their three cats.

Kristen Walker is an artist, giggle enthusiast, and educational website developer. She lives in Santa Barbara, California, with her husband, Andy; their wiggly Labrador Winnie-girl; and their striped tiger Meme. She keeps a blog at kristenwalker.com and loves to get comments and visitors.

Being a graphic designer and artist served **Kimi Weart** well during her wedding planning, as she got to have tons of creative fun with the details. She is a dabbler in all things visual: making art, designing children's books and wedding stationery, sewing costumes and pillows, and generally leaving art supplies everywhere. She and her husband, Paul Galloway, live in Brooklyn, New York, with their son, August; a sweet fat dog; and a feisty skinny cat. They also have a cabin upstate, where she gets to traipse through the woods and splash in a creek. She had so much fun with the details of her wedding that it sparked a new business: her company A Printable Press, www.printablepress.com.

Abby Wentworth is a career bleeding heart, having made educational nonprofits her business for nearly a decade. She firmly believes in equal education for all children and in boozy brunches, the power of baked goods, the empire of Oprah, and that perpetual underdog we call New Jersey. She married her partner, Seth, in June 2012 in Oklahoma. Abby and Seth's relationship has weathered two pearl-clutching scenarios. First, they met on a free online dating site (oh my!) and lived to tell the tale. Second, shortly thereafter and on somewhat of a lark, Seth packed up his life in Oklahoma and moved to Hoboken to be with Abby (and to kick-start a career in comedy, but let's dwell in the romanticism please). They're living happily, complexly, thoughtfully, and honestly ever after.

Sarah W-W and her soon-to-be wife, Catherine, are planning a secular wedding with dashes of Jewish tradition to be held in Provincetown, Massachusetts. They live in Boston with their two cats, Mitzi and Maddow. While their wedding won't have the $2,000 price tag, it will have the $2,000 spirit of sanity and reasonableness. Both brides plan to keep their names. (Negotiations regarding the last names of any potential offspring of this union are in process.) Sarah blogs occasionally about her undying love of food at http://www.stalkingsarah.com.

INDEX